THE REAL SOLDIER

SAMSON AGBOOLA

TABLE OF CONTENT

THE REAL SOLDIER

ACKNOWLEDGMENTS

With deep gratitude and loyalty I have the honor to express my appreciation to the following for their contributions:

To Rear Admiral Goddy A. Anyankpele, for believing in the idea of 'The Real Soldier' and attesting to its value, for this sir I am immensely grateful beyond words.

A philosopher wrote "opportunity is missed by most because when it comes knocking it is dressed in Coverall and looks like work thus they never let it in" so I appreciate Rear Admiral Adeniyi A. Osinowo for all his many lessons, and for been a mentor to me during these times.

To Commodore Abimbola O. Ayuba for all his advices, parables and seeing to my enrollment in the transformation course which today form a vital part of my life and this book. As a sage sir, your kind words of wisdom never fell on deaf ears.

To Commodore AC Unoneme who with great personal sacrifice saw my manuscript to perfection, his will, tenacity and selflessness is an inspiration to many young individuals like myself trying to climb the ladder of success. And also to lieutenant MS Abbas, Seaman Collins and Miss Ugbede Okwoli who all contributed to the editing of this book.

To Commodore EA Ogbonnaya for her guidance and helpful insights, To lieutenant Commander MA Kolo, and Sub lieutenant OJ Egbelo for their counsel in the course of this project.

To all my Commanding Officers and instructors who have all contributed in grooming me, to especially Captain OA Daniels a great teacher who inspired me dearly.

To Dr Kayode Taiwo head of psychology department Lagos state university for all his encouragement, support and the devotion of his time to seeing this book to fruition. And also Dr Lawal for his advices along the way and the entire department of psychology Lagos state university.

To my esteemed colleagues, Petty Officer Ogunfolaju and Seaman Emokpae Rufus for our many conversations which proved helpful to this book. To Seaman Ekele Ochinoku Micheal our time in the down-below galley of NNS Erinomi " truly thought provoking" Seaman Akolo John Magga a devoted friend, AB Ameh D aka gbhoshi, Seaman Ahmeed and Seaman Opute.

To Seaman Ehiozuwa Bonaventure and wife who helped put together a study group during the initial stages of this book, Seaman Ibede Felix, Seaman Randolph Uza, Seaman Osewengie and Seaman Mohammed SM.

To my beloved wife and daughter, for enduring my absence of both mind and body throughout the journey, for showering me with love, support and encouragement. To my mother and brothers for being there for me and to Kunle whose encouragement, advice and support have elevated greatly my writing dream.

To all the officers and men of Headquarters Naval Training Command Apapa Lagos may God's hand of favor never depart from you all. Last and not the least: I beg forgiveness of all those who have been with me over the course of the years whose names I have failed to mention.

FOREWORD

My initial contact with 'The Real Soldier' gave the impression of a novel or work of fiction until I began to 'explore' it and it became clear that the book is an expose of the personality of some human beings with special focus on the military profession. This book therefore is a product of human ethology (study of human behavior), borne out of the author's special interest in humanism, especially his concerns with the needs, wellbeing and interest of 'the Soldier' having grown up in the Barracks.

The Author revealed that lack of self-realization of individual traits and personalities early in life, especially among the youths which constitute a great percentage of the workforce, has been the bane of many societies. Thus, a lot of young men and women are misguided and have been set off-track while others are moving against 'the tide of life' as far as their destinies are concerned.

I see the 'The Real Soldier' as an attempt by Agboola to contribute his quota in assisting young men and women to address the protracted issues of realizing their 'personalities' and steering a safe course to their destinies. The Book identifies the 7 common types of personality, their blends and characteristics, and unfolds the strengths and weaknesses inherent in each personality type. Readers will find its unique style quite interesting and captivating as it traces the timeless truth of the role of the family, the society and environment in shaping various personality types and provides practical recipes and nuggets to enable people to self-realize which personality type/blend they belong to. The author also provides answers for those that would like to make good choices in relationships and tips on how people should manage their weaknesses and maximize their strengths to be the best they could be. For authorities and leaders in charge of organizations, especially the military, Agboola gives insight on how to know your personnel, understand them and effectively make choices of the personality types/blends best suited for various assignments, tasks and deployments. This is an excellent aspect of the book that could enhance the human resource management of the military. More so that he recommended the establishment of military rehabilitation Centre for personnel with alcohol and drug related issues. In reflection, I perceive 'The Real Soldier' does not only apply to military personnel, but to the larger civilian populace as well. Therefore, given the occasional strained relationship between the military and the civil populace, this book can serve as a bridge to address the gaps that often border on perceptions and interpersonal relations. Thus, 'The Real Soldier' is a 'must read' for all young men and women who desire to discover themselves especially the hidden and ignored creative power they possess which could enable them reach their desired future.

If you are in this category, I believe that you will find this book highly inspiring and unforgettable, like you will realize that you have more control of your life and destiny as you never imagined.

I congratulate Agboola Samson Oluwatosin for this great work. Thank you for contributing to human capacity development in the Military and in the larger civil society.

Rear Admiral Goddy Ambah Anyankpele
GSS psc[+] AOWC Msc FCIS

PART 1

ANGLES OF THE THEORY

.

Sometime ago, during my recruitment exercise into the Nigerian Navy, I sat down with a group of recruits and we were all pointing out why we wanted to join the military. *The* *Caustic* was the first to respond. He stated, "Too many a time I have been dealt with by men in uniform, therefore, I must wear this uniform." The *Conceit* with a stern look said, "This is my father's job and I too must do it." *The*

Service-Chameleon quickly interrupted him, smiled and said, "I just love the white and white uniform and want to wear it also." *The* **Austere***,* with a look of resolve and a calm exterior said, "I want to use the military influence to elevate myself, imagine the things I can do with a military identity." *The* **Repressed** with a look of self-pity said, "We live in difficult times and the military pays better." Then there was a moment of silence. The Caustic with an aggressive tone now broke the silence and asked the Timorous. "Is your tongue on strike?" Then *The* **Timorous** simply sighed and said, "I do not know, it is my uncle that bought the Navy form for me."

Before entry into the military service, the civil life of every personnel goes a long way in influencing who he is, and who he becomes in the service. Over the period of service, the exposures that are characterized with the military have their effects, but they are not as domicile as those before personnel joined the service.

This personality theory as it relates to members of the armed forces is a theory that stipulates the different kinds of personalities within the other ranks cadre. The theory can be linked to their lives before service and how their current exposures regulate them. It analyzes in details how the different personality types influence each soldier, rating or aircraftman in different ways; determining their level of efficiency and dedication and the way they relate with other personnel coordinate their lives, run their families, and plan for retirement. It also analyzes how these influences affect their lives in general terms, both positively and negatively; how to deal with the negative ones and improve the positive aspects. It applies to every individual, both the military and the civil populace; its application is thus in three angles- the officers, the soldiers and civilians.

FOR OFFICERS

From the initial training and onward development, the military high command has made it a point of importance that the average officer should have what it takes to know his men. An officer should be able to interact with his men and at the same time understand their most influencing factors. It is indeed a fact that all officers are equipped with this knowledge; but at what level is this information or knowledge part of the paradigm through which the officers take charge of their subordinates? It is noteworthy that the true 'color' of personnel is often subdued by many factors relating to life and service exigencies. It is only at intervals that the true 'colors' of a soldier, rating, or aircraftman are noticed. His past influences what he is now and how that interferes with his output in the service, within his command or unit. Thus, this theory is a vivid reminder of what is inherent and intrepid insight into whom we are as soldiers, our fears and shortcomings, and the way out. The understanding of this theory would enable any officer make tactical decisions without undermining morale. Thus, giving his men what an officer ought to in terms of appropriate guidance. This in return would enhance efficiency, facilitate unswerving loyalty and boost morale.

FOR SOLDIERS, RATINGS, AND AIRCRAFTMEN

In the world of today, education of the mind and elevation of intellectual ability have become necessities preached in equality to certain religious tenets. This trend is also domicile in the military arena as most soldiers, ratings, and aircraftmen struggle to be educated despite the tight routine of the military vocation. In all ramifications of these studies, our primary duty remains our service to the armed forces, the success of which is based largely on a soldier's, rating's and aircraftman's relationship with his colleagues and his understanding of himself. Individual search for knowledge in different angles of life will not touch majorly and intricately at other ranks that live in the barracks. The personality theory X-rays our challenges in the service and how they interfere with our outputs in our ships, units or establishments, our personal lives, our family lives and our future especially after service. Thus, the theory is a good way to come to terms with all these and understand them on a more vivid note. Therefore, the soldier who not only reads but also assimilates and reflects is regarded a better soldier, rating, or aircraftman, for himself, his family, individual service, and country.

FOR CIVILIANS

Apart from certain civilians privileged to have had close contact with service personnel over an extended period, the civil population has always viewed the soldier, from a distance, as an animal, unsocial, uncivil, unconventional, and unlearned human being. This is a trend that sprouts from lack of knowledge of the real soldier, who is a human just like every other human being, with fears and limits. Civilians mostly, due to the rigidity of military edicts and the classified nature surrounding military activities, have been deprived the opportunity to deal with this ignorance. They therefore, judge in accordance with what they see and hear. This therefore, is an apt opportunity for the average civilian to understand the life and challenges of the real soldier.

THE COMPONENTS

In recent times, studies regarding psychological classification and personality traits identify factors such as social background, environment, and political situation as secondary influencers of inherent traits in man. Theories like that of Tim Lahaye and others have it that, the human temperament is passed on genetically. Tim further classified them, into four distinct groups, namely, the sanguine, choleric, melancholy and phlegmatic. In analyzing the personality of a soldier, while the genetically passed on trait remains paramount, other secondary influences such as social background, environment and political situation come into play. The inherited personality traits from our genetic lines serve as the bedrock for the psychological output of each personnel. However, the traits are not the distinguishing factors in analyzing the soldier's personality in this book.

The soldier's personality as described in this book has taken into considerations many factors. These factors make up the actual paradigm that makes a soldier who he is and the resultant actions he displays. Therefore, irrespective of genetically inherited personality, the paradigms through which a soldier views life as a soldier, rating or aircraftman are first established in the 'Components' mentioned earlier. Those are what determine the actual personality of a soldier.

In this chapter, I shall consider briefly the six (6) Components that serve as a build- up to whatever personality category a personnel falls into. These 'Components' are what characterize the qualities of every personality that will be described in the subsequent chapters.

The following are the components;

1. *Family background*

2. *Social integration*

3. *Religious affiliation*

4. *Physicality*

5. *Educational strength / intellectuality*

6. *Environment.*

FAMILY BACKGROUND

The family background of every personnel, serves as leading factor that categorizes the personality type under which a personnel belongs. Everyone has different family background which is all based on where a personnel originates from. It might be a polygamous or monogamous home, with a member of an extended family, different foster homes, uncles or aunties, religious homes, Refugee camps, orphanage etc. *Conceits* have actual parents that they grew up with (father or mother that serves in the military or a close family member that does) which in the process of their childhood may or may not have assumed their responsibility as parents to them. Their family backgrounds are mostly characterized by hardship and struggles; they actually strived to get hold of things. In rare cases conceits have families of average rating; but if any conceits come from this line, they are either considered outcast or their parents do not see too much value in them.

The *Caustic* may be from an actual family, but even in that case he grew up hating his parents or guardians, their decisions, the outcomes of his life and many related factors. The *Repressed* did not grow up with their actual parents; they grew up either with foster care or with an extended family member, or relative. They mostly went through a great deal in life that inhibited them from what they thought they were supposed to get from their real parents. The

Service Chameleon is similar to the Conceit in family background; the difference between both is that, the families of the service chameleon do not have military tie. The *Timorous* comes from an actual family, or was raised by an extended family member, or even relatives that assumed full responsibility of their upbringing. They were provided with all the necessities as children, but were not loved, or accepted by a leading member of the family they grew up with (that is 'the father or mother figure'). The *Austere* has an actual family, but even with his family, he had to struggle to make ends meet under the supervision of his parents. This is probably due to responsibilities that the family put on him.

The *Euphoric* can come from any of these backgrounds.

SOCIAL INTEGRATION

The *Conceit* had an active social life throughout childhood from either what happened around him, or what he was actively involved in. The *Repressed* exhibits a total lack of conventional social integration, but mostly a traditional sense of sociality. The *Caustic* observed social activities from a distance; but due to factors such as his bizarre nature, poverty, the ground rules of his parents or guardians which he had to endure, he never really got a taste of sociality. The *Service Chameleon* had a minimal level of social activities. The *Timorous* watched and observed social activities, but lacked the physiological maturity and parental push to integrate. The *Austere* in most cases were privileged to lead an active social life, but choose not to. The *Euphoric* can range from any of the above.

RELIGIOUS AFFILIATIONS

Conceits are always prompt as an obligation either to mosque or churches, as the case may be. However, they may choose not to attend at all or to attend only occasionally.

Repressed are not religious in nature, but always reverence God.

Caustics are not in the least religious; sometimes it becomes difficult to tell what faith they represent. The *Service Chameleons* are very religious and take pleasure in religious activities. The *Timorous* are religious and lead a spiritual life to compliment. The *Austere* is only religious out of obligation. The religious nature of the *Euphoric* depends on the trends of time and his personal emotions.

ENVIRONMENTAL FACTORS

The *Conceit* grew up in a classical military urban environment, either a barracks or an environment close to a barracks. The *Repressed* grew up in a typical rural area. The *Caustic* may have grown up in a rural area, but has a touch of civilization in his upbringing. The *Service Chameleon* grew up in an urban area. The *Timorous* may come from an urban or rural environment as the case may be. The *Austere* is the same as the Timorous, while the *Euphoric* could be any of the above.

PHYSICALITY

The *Conceit* is a natural narcissist, who looks young and good. The *Repressed* on enlistment are normally over aged, looking wrinkled or old. The *Service Chameleon* has similarity with the conceit, but they are not narcissistic in nature. The *Austere* is physically average. The *Caustic* may look good or wrinkled, but whatever their physicality represents to themselves, it is not good enough. The *Euphoric* looks pale, sickly, and malnourished.

EDUCATIONAL STRENGTH/INTELLECTUALITY

The *Conceit* is an O'level holder i.e. high school or secondary school, and mostly possesses an average or very high 1Q, with a minimal level of self-confidence. *Repressed* is advanced beyond high school, obtaining diploma, NCE, or its equivalent. That is why mostly they are over aged and those that do not obtain academic diploma or its equivalent are skilled in a professional handwork. The IQ of the Repressed is always lacking compared to the level of his academic qualification. The *Caustic* does not join the military by choice. They mostly have spent several years exploring other minor vocations before enlistment; it is his years of experience that make him appear smart, forward, and seemingly ambitious. They are O'level holders with average IQ. The *Service Chameleon* and the *Timorous* are either, holders of O'level or diploma, or their equivalent. Those that completed high school were enlisted within the age range, and those that have obtained diploma enlist after their certification. They possess either an average IQ or below.

The *Austere* are O'level holders, and are as a rule clever. They are the most confident among the group, with IQ above average, or very high. The *Euphoric* can be any of the above.

SPECIAL CONSIDERATIONS

In one of my books titled Mortality Reason Religion. I illustrated that upon birth, a child is just like a vast memory chip, void of anything, free and waiting to be loaded with information, details, history, experiences, knowledge, etc. The process through which this information enters his mind, the kind of details that he receives, his upbringing, his immediate environment, parental influences, and most of all, the entire political situation in the country, in their overall sense determine to the largest extent the future of such a child. I will analyze these factors majorly in this theory of the soldiers' personality. In addition, these factors constitute what form the paradigm that determines the personality of a soldier. There are also some cases that may be different and may not conform to the theory in this book. Such cases are the ones, that remarkable changes have been registered in the personnel's personality, thereby altering whom they were for either better or worse. Furthermore, cases as such normally express themselves in time and experience and are common among senior non-commissioned officers where time has altered who they were. A *Reformed Conceit* is one that comes to terms with his extravagance, narcissism, and excess socialization due to time and experience and expresses a kind of humility that is benevolent in nature. On the other hand, a Service *-Chameleon* is one that has learnt to believe in himself, expressing confidence in his own actions, irrespective of people's opinions. In some cases, it can be factors as religion/morality where a *Caustic* finds himself embracing a spiritual life or moral standard just to fulfill a twisted course. If that is the case, his Caustic nature will still be present in his religious expression, pushing his morality to the extreme. However, if he found spirituality on a transcendent ground he becomes an alteration of his former self. Such a case as this can apply to any of the personalities described in this book. That is because the very factors that classify a personnel into any of the seven personalities, are factors that were adapted from childhood through to maturity influencing their output and responses in distinct ways. They are not genetic factors that can only be repressed, but can under stronger influence and with proper motivation be overcome. A Euphoric with a God fearing, decent wife, who influences him positively, can later come to see the light. Also, even with motivation and support of the military authority through extensive counseling and rehabilitation, a *euphoric* personnel can be transformed beyond recognition. On the other hand, a *Conceit* with a bad wife or acquaintances can be pushed to a euphoric status. So it should be noted that apart from the root Components mentioned earlier, a personnel's personality can be altered because of any, or more of the factors mentioned above.

In conclusion, the soldiers' personality theory is based on my life growing up in the barracks, specifically Sam Ethan Air force base Ikeja Lagos Nigeria. Learning and observing the lives of elders and uncles, watching closely their successes, failures, what characterized their pains, regrets as well as their joy and fulfillment, until I became a member of the Nigerian armed forces in the Navy. Through my years in the service, I have taken a keen interest in understanding my fellow soldiers, through both my experience, those of others, research and extensive study. This is because understanding what prompts a soldier's action is a gateway to complete harmony within colleagues, without a misunderstanding of motives. Furthermore, it will be observed that throughout this book references were only made with masculinity, which is because in the military setting all are regarded as males. It is based on all these that I have come to propose this theory being a writer myself, and having published two titles earlier. I have put my little experience, research, and studies into this book, and with continuous support of my beloved wife who shares the same background, my course mates and friends. However, I believe that as this book is in its first edition it may not be perfect or conclusive, but there is a lesson inherent, to be learnt by both civilians and personnel in the armed forces.

PART 2

THE PERSONALITY TYPES

THE AUSTERE

Look around your unit and observe that there are personnel whose outside lives are always interfering with their work, through either their business cliques or ambition to quickly graduate and become officers. The point here is they never rely totally on the military for their livelihood or those of their families.

The Austere make up about 10% of the other ranks cadre and on enlistment are

O'level holders within any age range. Their ambition is boundless and unconceivable, because given every opportunity, they have a very high tendency to intimidate others and boast their egos using their achievements. This trait is on the high side. The Austere is a stern service personnel, who believes in justice rather than mercy and where justice is not executed, he gets irritated. He is neat and follows the rules and his standard of excellence is so great that he himself cannot meet up. The Austere is goal driven and is rarely influenced by the exigencies of the service. In whatever unit he finds himself, prior to reporting he has already mapped out all he wants to achieve and the possible ways of achieving them. He does not believe his life should be based solely in the military. Most of them have other businesses and connections that fund their activities, and always achieve their ways by hook or crook no matter the price. They will betray any one to achieve their means, and not just betrayal, a calculated one at that. Their plans are always well analyzed, because they are actually brilliant or clever and do not look back if they have set their minds on something. That is why sometimes they are mistaken for Caustics, but when you take a closer look, you will observe the distinction. Their higher-activities influence comes to fore, when they are either the Regimental Sergeant Major, Chief Boatswain Mate, CSM or Bofor of a Ship or Establishment (leadership positions of the other ranks cadre). You do not want to step on their toes, because this type will frustrate you. They share this characteristic with the caustic that can sometimes be forgiving. Their loyalty goes with necessity irrespective of rank or appointment. Most personnel from the eastern and sometimes southern part of Nigeria fall into this category. Frugality is their watchword, and when it comes to socialization, they love and crave for it, but express it only strategically. They possess very weak conscience, and always make the greatest enemy to the Conceit, whom they always feign to be friendly with. Although the Conceit may not come out openly to the Austere, to talk about their frugality and meanness, these are usually topics for discussion when the Austere is absent. They have a weakness for the opposite sex; In fact, their greatest loophole is the opposite sex. The Austere are extremely intuitive individuals and make excellent leaders. Once in leadership position, the first wings they like to clip are those of the Conceits, because they are the only personality that can actively cause disharmony in their leadership. In totality, the Austere is a proud man, a consummate manipulator, ambitious beyond rationality who gloats on other people's failure, and whose conscience has long gone to sleep. His success is his happiness, and if he finds happiness in family, it is only when the family expresses the same success he feigns.

THE CAUSTIC

The Caustics are the easiest to identify among the group, plainly, because they hardly hide their feelings no matter how wicked it might sound, or how negatively it might affect another personnel. They are often referred to as sadists. The Caustics make up about 10% of service personnel, over aged on enlistment, mostly looking wrinkled and unattractive with intellectuality on an average level. Before a personnel falls under this category, it does not just happen. There is always an event, a circumstance, in the past, features about him so glaring that differentiate him from what he feels he ought to be or have been. When you take a closer look at these people, you find out that their parents or a loved one suffered from the hands of the society when they were much younger and the effect has become so devastating to them in such a way that it looks as though they want to give back to the society. To every Caustic, there is always a downside or connection in his past or in his physicality that feeds his bitterness. This deficiency can be physical, psychological, educational etc. Most of them had childhood experience where the social elites constantly ostracized them, or they were not loved enough during their childhood or did not experience what it is to be loved. The Caustic has a twisted mind that makes him inclined to be negative in his words and actions, objecting to positivity, but succumbs only under numeral or veto pressure. It is common to hear them talk about what is right and obtainable, how personnel should express discipline, forthrightness etc. They are very aggressive enforcers and possess weak conscience. The Caustic is a paranoid soldier, trusting no one even himself. Since they feign discipline, they avoid criticisms by all means; especially by the authority so they are always prompt to work and obedient in carrying out their duties. They hardly criticize authority, only when the authority does not approve of their sadistic nature. The Caustic has a long-standing vendetta against the Conceit who is prone to socialization, can be carefree, and when placed above them will always put them on a very short leash. Furthermore, in all his sadistic nature, the Caustic can be an intellectual, and mostly reasonable if you abide by his strict rules. Fun and socialization in his standard are the height of indiscipline. That is why the Caustics can be loners when it comes to sociality and can push themselves beyond means. Caustics also have a high appeal for the opposite sex but are very secretive in its expression. I remember a story in Machiavelli's version of Cesar Borgia's campaign under his father Pope Alexander Borgia. In the late fifteenth century, where the people of a town named Romagna were lawless and defiant, Cesar used an aggressive brute named Messer Ramiro d'orco to pacify the town enforcing law and order in the cruelest and harshest form until law and order was instilled in the town. That is the most effective role of the Caustics, because they would not take lightly on indiscipline so long as the authority supports them. In addition, they will equally give their unswerving loyalty to whoever is willing to tolerate their lack of pity and sadistic nature.

The caustic has a weakness, which everyone sees, and as such, he tries to put up a defense mechanism for his weakness. He is an extremist and a pretender. He has set a standard and does not want to break it, even in the face of what he truly wants. He has portrayed himself as an upright man in the face of all. However, when he is in the place where no one knows him he displays his true self, which is always on the extreme. To him, service is all about discipline. He cautions every body's children and in most cases, his own children are the ones getting it wrong and being in troubled spots or situations.

These classes of people are selfish to their families, very greedy and always want to use power to take from others and never want to give. They prefer to give only when they will be spotted. They always want to be perfect in the eyes of everyone. They take delight in disseminating bad news.

In time of retirement people do not come to him for anything, and his family is not satisfied with his achievement. He knows too much and ends up ruining things for himself. Sixty percent of this group does not have a fulfilled retirement life; they are dissatisfied with what they have achieved, and tend to blame it on others especially those who try to help them with advice.

THE CONCEIT

To a Conceit, soldering is a way of life and indeed the best way to live. He is determined to be an achiever in his capacity. His overall conduct is a distinctive feature he alone possesses. When a civilian gets close to a conceit, he will indeed be tempted to join the service. Out of service, the conceit seems to have an average but seemingly fulfilled life. He tells his service stories especially his success story to as much that care to listen. In addition, even at this point, he still wants to set the pace for others to follow; he is a satisfied man and never regrets the fact that he was a soldier, even if he does not make an officer. He has had it all good- life, socialization, asset and even the women. They make up about 28% of the other rank cadre, and most personnel that fall under this category seem to be very satisfied with their present state. They do not want to push too hard. He tries to see the end from the beginning and of course, in most cases he gets discouraged especially when he foresees hurdles ahead. He never leaves his comfort zone and does not trade it for anything. He prefers to be where he is with minimal challenges and risk, than leaving to a place where he will be confronted with greater challenges and risk.

The conceit is that egocentric military personnel, that understand the basic concept of the military life before enlistment, hardly enlist as over aged, mostly due to parental and environmental influences. Throughout their early lives, they had the chance to view firsthand what it takes to be a rating, soldier, or an aircraftman. Most of them, during their childhood swore never to work that path, but upon maturity are forced to choose between two lesser demons. However, those that choose the life of personnel have harbored within them a secret need to be officers. The conceit sees his time in service as a calling, as a need to fulfill an ancestral connection, or of whatever influence the past might have had on him in relation to this. When Conceits are not able to be officers, initially due to circumstances beyond their powers, they harbor a need to be one, which is accompanied with a concrete plan. For the few that do not possess the ambition to push eventually live out their time as successful soldiers, ratings and aircraftmen, and see to it that their dreams to become officers are eventually fulfilled in the life of one of their offspring's. The conceit is proud with a good sense of humor that can be reasonable. They are natural narcissist and look neat and sharp to work. They devote their time and energy to the service, and are major influencers of what the service gives to them. They do not allow the exigencies of the service to affect their personal and family lives and are very smart about it. The groups that mostly influence their posting/draft are conceit. They like to be in control mostly because they are in one educational outfit or the other or simply because they will not want the armed forces to have so much influence on their lives. The conceit is naturally egocentric, in most cases, so they map out their duties and avoid embarrassment. They are the types that when given power to take charge like to delegate responsibilities to their subordinates, take pride in their rank/rate no matter how inferior it is. The conceit hardly belittles himself and is appreciated by officers who fall into this category. The conceits are O'level holders on enlistment, young and ready as the year's progress. Two things usually happen to them; either they actually achieve feats such as educational advancement, career building and property expansion, that helps build their much-needed confidence, or they fail in this, and conjure up alibi to cover their flaws, but still brag about how over achieved they are. Conceits are accurate braggers, except you are a fellow conceit, or very close to the conceit involved, their bragging will carry you away. Of how over achieved they are, and how life have been so perfect for them with a promising future to follow. In life, either the conceit is raised in a socially friendly environment or he is quick to learn from his environment. Moreover, conceits are in the habit of making friends within themselves, because other personality types will not be able to measure up to the kind of life they profess. They live a life of extravagance and heightened socialization. The conceit that manages to escape the trait only does so temporarily, as far as there are no other conceits together with which he will indulge in it. Once a fellow conceit comes along and they get to know each other, he enters the same pit. They love to live a lavish life that is above their means. They put themselves in the spotlight as being distinctive and over achievers, for other personnel to see them and tag them as 'officers in other ranks clothing'. This is the effect they want to create from their meager salary, which they have to share part sometimes with their siblings who well understand their life style. Conceit hardly indulges in illegality, and even though they are pushed to do so, they want to enter big time, play the big leagues. They are actually sharp critics of whoever is not neat, organized, engages in petty illegalities, or those that are easily bamboozled at the office. In actual sense, the conceit is the most civilized among the entire groups and does not help their leadership skills as long as it has to do with the military. Military organization and skills are not based on civility neither are they based on your high sense of humor nor socializing skills. It only makes you to be loved, cherished, and admired by those who cannot read between the lines. Therefore, conceit are mostly admired, praised, and envied in the office and for younger cases, other groups are in cue to be their friends. The conceit has between an average or minimal IQ his integrity is strongest amongst the personality types, and they have the highest level of loyalty that is based solely on their own decision. Most conceits are extrovert and the few that are not, have suppressed theirs to a high level.

The conceits are naturally generous and are the most compassionate of the entire groups. They have the ability to understand other personnel's troubles and are also willing to help. In the face of danger, the conceit can be highly tensed and emotional and if the scenario drags on, they achieve and gain control over their emotions.

THE EUPHORIC

Your children are always the last to go to school and the first to come back home; most times they are driven for coming late or for school fees. Your boss gives your wife a percentage of your salary before giving you the balance. You always have a case with your family and always at Welfare or Regulating office to settle family issues. You are not a stranger in the cell, though you do not do anything wrong, people just fail to understand your personality. May be you are retired and your family refused to move with you. They are always revolting and antagonizing you. You give excuses for everything. Even now as you are reading this, you are still giving excuses. Early when I was recruited into the Navy, I was drafted to serve onboard a Corvette NNS ERINOMI. A negative gangway was declared (no going out) that coincided with when they just paid our salaries. On the evening of that day, the Officer of the Day cleared lower deck (that is to say all the hands should muster). When the strength was taken, one person was missing. Throughout the night he did not turn up. Three days after, he showed up, and when the Commanding officer interviewed him about his whereabouts and why he disobeyed the 'negative gangway' and went ashore. He simply said "I did not use the gangway to go out sir; I used the head – rope". Excuses, that is on a lighter note. Whichever location you are posted to, the Commander must know you one on one even before a month of resumption. From the day you joined the force, your parents have had cause to start calling your Commander to plead on your behalf. If all these are true about you, then you are indeed in this group.

Their wives have learnt to follow them the way they are. In most cases, they marry stubborn women, either a prostitute or the stubborn girls in their quarters. They do not marry officially, they either, impregnate a woman and she moves in with them, or their families impose a wife on them. Some of them die mysteriously; others do not get promotion for a long time. Some suffer de-ranking while those that are fortunate enough to disengage from service with their course mates, with their actual portfolio, do not always have anything to show for their years in service.

At the end of every month, there are always 'buying one Job' (Committing an offence) or the other; chronic drunks and drug addicts that is another word to use for them; always high on something. They drink every day and those that do not drink smoke Indian hemp and it is usually worse after salary has been disbursed. They make up about 8% of the other rank cadre. The primary desire of the euphoric is to keep his mind intoxicated, he is the biggest debtor, and most of their debts are owed in bars and 'Ogogoro Joints' (where locally made spirits are sold). They start drinking from the start of day and continue until either fund runs out or the seller is unwilling to sell more credit. They have no discipline to the extent to which they drink. These types are disconnected from their families; it mostly takes intervention before they drop welfare money for their battered wives and tattered children. In some cases, they happen to be intellectually sound, and when they are high with their words, they can elevate a depressed soul. No matter the circumstance, they are always happy irrespective of the problem they face and their numerous debts. They have a high propensity for prostitutes and most of them end up marrying prostitutes as wives, and a knack for trouble accompanies them everywhere they serve. In whatever ship or unit they are, you can always single them out for one problem or the other. Sometimes they just go missing for days even weeks, or immediately after salary is paid and when the money is exhausted they run back to base as innocent as ever. Funny enough, the service tolerates them because such action will never be condoned coming from another group. Like I said before, they are always happy and satisfied and there is always a glow in their appearance, the only thing that dulls out the light is when they cannot satisfy their euphoria. The euphoric talks and assume himself a lawyer, and no matter what offence they commit, they have one justification or the other; they have termed themselves smart individuals. These types have little or no concern for themselves, their health, or that of their children. They are always influenced by the trend of the current moment, without a vision for the possible future. They always speak out of turn; in any parade or muster, they serve as sources of concern to every other group. Their socialization which is hyperactive, and the constant need to be around mind-altering agents always make them very feeble physically, and prone to experience physical degeneration. The euphoric are always victims of service exigencies and may seem docile and without ambition, but have charted always short distant goals.

THE TIMOROUS

Two things always standout about the Timorous;   other officers and personnel fight their battles, because their humility intrigues them. Secondly, in whatever establishment they serve, they are always praised for their good character, discipline, commitment, and loyalty. The timorous make about 12% of the other ranks cadre. On enlistment, they can be either O'level or diploma holders. They are quiet, humble, and they carry out all orders and even those that are not military, to avoid trouble. Sometimes their juniors tend to control them and they will most times willingly take it to avoid a hassle. They hate anything that will bring them to the spotlight. They always like to observe or act from the background. These types are long-suffering, calm, and slow to anger and can endure hardship or maltreatment without actively complaining. They value their jobs as service personnel not because it is the only resort; on the contrary they tend to be too scared of changing their career. These types possess the highest level of fear among all the personality types, and the lowest level of confidence because they can hardly speak for themselves. They are generally slow individuals and when it comes to sociability, they are misfits in this aspect and rarely socialize. They are prudent spenders and wise planners of their personal life; in fact, they have the best personal life compare to other personalities, because they are peaceful and make excellent family men if not wrongly influenced. The timorous are easily influenced individuals who will succumb to pressure of a stubborn Austere, or a smart Caustic and will make excellent puppet for them. They are viewed as slackers and are often over used by the hierarchy. These types always follow the rules and will not, under normal circumstances disobey an order. The timorous has little or no affinity to acquire knowledge or increase his academic wealth, except if influence by a close person who has the ambition. They may seem visionless and without ambition; but they are vipers with greatest of ambition. When given a leadership position it will seem as if his advisers are influencing him; but in real sense, he is running things as he best sees fit. The timorous are overly loyal, and they do not attach sentiment to their loyalty when expressed and are often viewed as misguided loyalist. When angered, which is very rare, the timorous can be very dangerous and unstoppable, his calmness might turn into the sadistic nature of the caustic, and one will wonder what changed. The timorous can make good acquaintance if not taken for granted as they are normally done.

These groups of people are extremists; their humility is on the extreme so also their anger. They make good team leaders, as they always carry people along, they do not just give orders, they also take part in implementing the orders to make sure nothing is left undone. They are perfectionists because if given a task, they do not just execute but execute with excellent result or output. They have great understanding and compassion for their subordinate. People love to work with this group of people and can easily take advantage of their simplicity. He is a peacemaker, and will not mind serving other peoples punishment. You may misinterpret him to be weak, but alas! You do not wish to meet him on his bad day, because when he wants to be stubborn, people get scared, he goes to the extreme.

He has a wonderful family; about 80% of them have wonderful families, they are indulgent with their children giving them proper discipline, except the unfortunate ones who marry strange women that destroy their homes, and leave, forcing them to live a life of pity. Little wonder, they are very careful in making choices, they tend to be confused in the face of multiple options. This is just to avoid mistakes, as they do not want problem.

They are not risk takers and are always satisfied with their comfort zone. Whenever you see them taking risk or doing something differently, look deep you will find out that someone they respect, love or trust have guaranteed them a favorable result to that effect. His family is his major priority. Thus after retirement he makes sure that, his family gets a very comfortable life.

They are highly emotional; as such their past failures can hold them down for a lifetime. Their greatest fear is in making decision because they are afraid of failure. They are excellent fathers and husbands; hence have almost a perfect family set-up. These types, the service actually fights for them and in the end, their timidity becomes a blessing in disguise.

Are you the timorous person? You have to learn to do things differently and try taking risk, stay positive, your carefulness and hard work are strengths which when channeled to the right direction can give you a fulfilled and almost perfect life as a service and ex-service man.

THE SERVICE-CHAMELEON

Most times the service chameleons are mistaken for the conceit because they have similar features that are visible, and they make up about 20% of the other rank's cadre. For instance, the service chameleons are not over aged on enlistment and they are O'level holders like the conceit. They are neat and express themselves confidently; they are socially average and most times good-looking. Nevertheless, there is a big difference between the service chameleon and the conceit. The service chameleon is a natural adapter irrespective of his ego; he is not principled as to which direction his life or career will take but guides it in accordance to what the service expects from him. Now, who is a service chameleon? A service chameleon is that armourer or engineer that is recalled from retirement because he is too good at what he does. He is that soldier, rating, or aircraftman that is neat and astute to work but never takes pleasure in his neatness or astuteness. In a new ship or unit, the service chameleon observes first, he fishes out the expectancies of the unit. Those that are respected in the units and immediately adapt and conform to all the expectancies of their units. A service chameleon befriends and copies the characters and attributes of those respected soldiers and offers himself in service and skills to the leading officers. Believe me when I say they are always good at what they do no matter their branch or specialization and are excellent copycats as far as the service is concerned. They can give the highest rate of high service so long as the leading officer likes and approves it. These types are excellent and shrewd observers and they do these mostly sub-consciously. It does not mean that they are always highly disciplined or neat. For instance, if a service chameleon finds himself in a unit where there is no discipline or the discipline is not enforced, and the leading and respected figures in the unit are indiscipline and probably the CO does not show interest in those acts, he will quickly adapts himself to be indiscipline as the leading figures. The service chameleon always sides with the winning team; if you are a loser or you are always criticized at work, he can never be your friend. Whatever establishment they serve at one point or the other, they are always praised. Because they easily adapt to the trends of the command and re- shape their psychological bearing to conform to it, if they cannot, they do so for a short period and excuse themselves. They can relate with any of the categories as far as it is among the winning team. They are mostly admired by the Caustic in power because they seem to conform to their view when necessary and to the austere because they are actually good at what they do and are quick learners. He tends to know everything that happens in his unit. They are the first amongst their mates to drive car(s) or own house(s). They see possibilities in every unit they find themselves. These types have high affinity for crime related trends; in fact, they actually enjoy it when it comes to looting and embezzlement, and make-good with a well-planned cover-up. If they are good at adapting and observing they are excellent pretenders.

When it comes to a cover-up, most times the authority as individuals, or senior officers feel more confident in letting them in on some dark secrets or on issues and activities they will prefer privately carried out. One down side of the service chameleon that later becomes glaring is that their loyalty depends on your scoreboard. They are the type that stabs in the back and when you turn to look at them, they are smiling at you. They never accept openly their status as chameleon and will argue it to the last. They are average spenders and even in face of their heightened social activities, they have mapped out what will cover their necessities. They are not civilized naturally but when they adapt to be civilized when necessary, it becomes obvious they feign it. When in power, the service chameleons make bad leaders, because they have been so carried away imitating others that they have no face or principle of their own. Their flexibility to learn, change and adapt becomes a disadvantage in the face of leadership. However, they are good followers, as long as the leader is not labeled a failure, but is revered or respected. The average service chameleon makes – up what is actually needed to be a good soldier.

THE REPRESSED

The repressed makes about 12% of Nigeria Armed Forces personnel. The repressed service personnel are always over aged for their rank. Their early life is characterized by struggle and childhood of ostracism from the average child. Throughout life, they have given up on the need to fill among as average civilized humans. The lucky ones who have managed to earn first level diploma /NCE or its equivalent are very obnoxious. Some learn a trade in life, and when they finally become military personnel, it is not as a matter of choice, desire or a need to serve, it is just the need to survive that pushes them. Thus, in most cases the repressed is already married with children before being recruited into the service; and once they get that chance, they value it so well and will stoop as low as needed to keep the job. So, he is an over aged rating, soldier or Aircraft man who obeys every order, but when he sees a stubborn conceit, or service chameleon disregards authority, he tends to be haughty, wanting or wishing to follow suit but does not possess the psychological grounding to finish. The repressed always admires the conceits and has an intrinsic need to be with them but do not measure up. The repressed is a slow soldier, rating, or aircraftman with a diploma, who likes to socialize with the conceit, but after a one time outing, he withdraws back to his shell. This is mostly because he cannot just understand their vain way of life and extravagance. The only reason he will come out again after sometime and follow them is because he constantly possesses this need to belong, to dine with the perceived winner and to be what he did not have the chance to be in the past. Nevertheless, his past suffering will be too strong for such a lifestyle to overwhelm him. So the repressed is at least on the average level and will not spend too much to socialize. He is very prudent in spending and even in the face of human (mortal) distraction; his past suffering still rides over his mind/desires. He is very realistic and disciplined when it comes to lifestyle and socialization. The repressed are not very neat and organized personnel, their uniforms are either not properly ironed or starched, or they are looking rough and unkempt.

They are sly, unreliable with words and easily switch sides; their loyalty is always in doubt and if at all they feign it, then they must have viewed in distant a prize they see as achievable to them. They are excellent concealers of personal ambition. It is not uncommon to hear them talk about how evil and degenerative the officers cadre is and how they do not want to be one, or even be in any office of authority, or proceed to operations. They will go on to say how they are satisfied with their current status, when in truth they will scheme to be officers, to rise above others they admire or envy. The repressed possess a low level of extroversion and normally tag along the extrovert, and for those that have found their way, befriend only the timorous.

As a matter of fact, the repressed are not civilized, neither are they intellectuals, and they hardly suffer after retirement, or finish their salary before the month ends. They are not ashamed of venturing into business, no matter how belittling it might seem. The repressed might be seen to be living in poverty, and be criticized for that. However, they have enough to sustain them on that level for a considerable period, even if income ceases. This is unlike the conceit that either exhausts himself before the month ends or does not have an emergency saving in case of unforeseen circumstances. Most mature officers appreciate the repressed and normally give them a long leash, but they are intuitive enough to watch them closely. When it comes to leadership, the repressed let it all out their past inhibitions, their improvised lives and want their followers to follow suit. They become aggressive and later mellow back into their shell when it becomes hard to achieve. Under the leadership of the repressed, a service chameleon can at least manage but a conceit might be forced to look for posting elsewhere. This is because at that point whatever demon that is repressed in them is let loose and the real fox is seen in the open. It is hard for one so concerned about his career, reputation, or ego to be caught under such net. Therefore, the phony Conceits or the ambitious Austere who like to bribe and manipulate their ways will not pray for a repressed to be CBM, or RSM of their unit.

However, the repressed have some short comings in their psychological formation. His way of reasoning and overall performance, including attitude in service is tied to emotion; thus he possesses an unstable mind. He is always confused and this is why he finds it very difficult to meet up during drills and parades. He tries to manage his extended family, immediate family and in most cases, this affects his job output; He is confident in his failure and always apologetic and ready to learn.

THE SOLDIER'S PERSONALITY AND ITS BLENDS

In attempting to explain each group in the soldiers' personality, we have taken time to analyze, what influences each soldier's output, what the root factors are, that catalyze how he chooses to live his life, run his family, interact in the service and plan for retirement. These factors range from family background, environmental factors and education/intellectuality to religious nature, social integration, and physicality. The principality/government that runs the state is also an important factor in the whole process. Having explained the seven groups that form the soldier's personality types, it is therefore expected that at this point one should be able to identify which group defines him. However, the theory still extends much further because our nature is far too complex for one person to be 100% Austere or Euphoric or as the case may be. Therefore, it is in my understanding that each personnel has a combination of at least two of the personality types imbedded in him. Where one of the personalities may express dominance over the other which is recessive, the percentage of the dominance over the recessive, or as the case may be can be determined by the personnel himself and the influencing factors which are found in the Components discussed earlier. Personnel can either be Repressed-Caustic where the repressed status is dominant and the Caustic is recessive or Euphoric-Conceit, dominant and recessive respectively.

AUSTERE-CAUSTIC

The Austere Caustic has two things that are of equal priority to him; his job and his business; in the overall sense, he wants to be financially independent while retiring in his peak. From when he starts as a private soldier, he begins to plan for retirement. This blend normally retire well because, they set out their goal and follow it with enough discipline to the end. They are disciplined personnel who are skilled in their individual vocations; they rate their family high and provide proper support when necessary. They rarely socialize or mix with people. As a rule, they are reserved and keep to themselves but whenever they want to talk, or advise, they tend to base it not on their personal achievement but on the mistakes soldiers make during their service years. Whenever they finally decide to socialize, which is during festive periods, they do it to the extreme and most times cannot control the outcome of such. After that, it takes them a longer period before they feel comfortable to socialize again. They will not either hesitate to criticize whoever is not doing so well openly, financially or work wise, and would not do so while referring to their success. They might refer to another. An Austere-Caustic should have been a very capable leader, but for the fact that he is not a very straightforward person. He lacks integrity and feigns loyalty. Initially it may seem he has the interest of his colleagues, associates or subordinates at heart given the way he expresses his actions but in the long run it becomes obvious his own personal agenda is what motivates him. This interferes with whatever goodwill or confidence personnel might have in his ability. And this trend seems to follow him around. While those that would not judge based on words later get to common terms with this reality. The Austere-Caustic needs to learn to be a parent to all that look up to him, and as a subordinate, treating all as he would his own, cutting down on his criticism emphasizing more on fatherly words. No matter the difference, a subordinate appreciates a fatherly figure than a critiquing superior.

AUSTERE-TIMOROUS

Apart from the conceited, the Austere-Timorous is one blend that expresses a high propensity to be a commissioned officer. Their Austere nature, which is greatly pacified by a blend of Temerity, reduces largely their will to venture into business. Although they may have investments but nothing they have to handle personally. Their interest mostly lies in elevating their profile through education and connections. Most personnel in this blend, if they do not succeed in making officers, the more successful ones opt into politics. They possess great ambition in building a career and have with it the will and discipline to follow through. Right from enlistment, they begin to make their way through the ranks attending seminars, professional courses, all these outside the military. They invest money into elevating their minds and profiles; and until they reach the peak they desire, they do not stop. This blend because of the timorous part is an excellent concealer of his ambition. Although he is obviously ambitious, but the steps he takes towards that direction is known to him alone as he does not allow same to interfere with his job in the service. He is punctual to parades, musters, and properly dressed to work. He respects his superiors and carries out orders without complains as he expects from his subordinates. Some of the obvious weaknesses of the Austere-Timorous are his selfish nature and his intense secrecy in all he does. He wants to do all alone; even though others might have shown interest in his pursuit of certain courses, seminars and lectures he attends, he would cover it in secrecy and makes sure he alone gets the better of it. If he was loyal to you today as a corporal because he is a private, do not expect same tomorrow once he becomes your superior i.e. an officer, even as a friend. He will turn sides and bring you to your knees. His loyalty goes with necessity and what the times offer. His actions, discipline and current humility are as a result of his current status. These are actions he expresses only to his superiors or those above him. His ambition and selfishness gets in his ways, his family and interpersonal relationship. This blend hardly stay long enough to become RSM'S or CBM'S and even those that reach that point do not covet leadership position in the military as other ranks.

AUSTERE-SERVICE CHAMELEON

For every Austere, there is always a tendency towards materialistic things, power, etc. The Austere are plain, ambitious and at the same time selfish; and for the Austere-Service-chameleon, he personally has no interest in creating a business enterprises. His major interest lies in his duties in the service. This type serves from one operation to another or operational base to operational base. They do not just continue serving in such places because they work their posting or have godfathers, it is because most of them are actually operationally capable and have shown their expertise either in the field or in the office. They dedicate their time to making the best of their service years. Throughout their period of going on operations and serving on operational bases, they have accumulated wealth and property in different areas and have established their immediate families. Those of them that are of the infantry or seaman core, are not afraid of life or death situation, and will quickly volunteer to go. They possess military courage and are excellent boosters of morale as leaders. Those that are not soldiers in the operational line are in either one sensitive office or the other. They are there solely because of their experience and expertise that have earned them reputations that are unswerving even when their experiences are irrelevant. Outwardly, personnel generally revere and praise these types because they are considered as being generous, but would not take lightly to them being cheated. Inwardly people fear them and attribute their being alive after much life threatening operations or remaining in office after many postings and drafts, to a spiritual connection. Personnel may express inhibition in embarking on deadly operation with these types because they have many tales of soldiers dying or MIA (Missing in Action) in operations that they were actively involved in and them returning alive often without a scratch. It causes an irrational fear of same happening to them. The Austere-Service chameleon is not without flaws. This blend has a bad temper and an uncontrollable love for money. Their love for money is so great that they forget when they put it above their family. It is so obvious they no longer hide it.

CAUSTIC- CONCEIT

This blend carries with it the best leadership quality you can find in soldiers, ratings or aircraftmen. His excellence in leadership extends from his work to his family. Apart from being just leaders, they listen and when not in leadership position they are disciplined and carry out orders, but can be stubborn, if they sense you are pushing them or playing on their intelligence. This blend is both clever and intelligent. Their turnout is neat and hardly will you find them wanting without a rational explanation. If you are indiscipline you will have a continuous problem with this type. You will dislike their policies and hate their leadership. They live active social life that does not interfere with their work, and love to socialize with fellow personnel, especially their juniors. Whoever they socialize with, they have studied and certified such personnel to be disciplined. If such a person displays any act of indiscipline or flouts orders, they will use the carrot and stick approach. Such is their tactics even on those they work with, but if you are out rightly indiscipline, they will offer no consolation except you become ready to see the wrong of your ways. I emphasis on this blend as leaders because where ever they find themselves, they try to take control and try to put themselves in an office of power and when it comes to integrity this blend has the highest of it. The major flaws of this blend reflect in their emotions which they tend to express in an extreme level when stimulated. If they get angry, they take it to the extreme, sometimes altering caustic comment that will pose a negative effect on all the good they have done in the past. For those of them that drink alcohol, they sometimes overdo it for one reason or the other thereby exposing their innate weakness. When stimulated by circumstances this blend has no control.

They can over-love or over-hate harboring resentment for years in their mind, and the worst of their enemies is whoever challenges their authority or seems a rival to them when in leadership position. They will lash out exposing their want for power and need to be in control. What is greatly required of this blend is a proper management of his emotions.

CAUSTIC-TIMOROUS

These types are loners that take great pleasure in whatever is theirs, from personal clothing to their wives and children. They are core-selfish, and seem to appear neat, uniform starched and well ironed, and their boots shone the most. Nevertheless, when you view their outward appearance, it sparkles but lacks a touch of perfection. There will always be a loose end here and there. Either the uniform is too starched or the ironing is too severe. They know their job in whatever specialization they belong. Whatever applies to them, they set in order and make sure they do not have problem or confrontation with authorities. The timorous part of them pacifies their caustic nature, taming several tiny outbursts or expressions into one powerful one. If he has not had enough, he will continue and will not be tamed. No blend harbors resentment, the way the caustic-timorous does. He can keep you as enemy for years in his mind and outwardly be your friend. They hardly speak their minds and whatever is not of relative concern to them they avoid. In their personal lives, they tend to have everything they need, because they would not want anything that would make them turn to ask from another person. They are prudent spenders and even though they socialize or womanize, they do it in secret and you would never guess they are involved in such. They try hard to avoid the limelight or anything that will push them forward with regards to sociality. However, when they are CBM, RSM or an active leader, they easily mix emotion with work because this blend has bottled up within him many resentments and emotions that he does not let out, and this greatly affects his leadership ability. The Caustic-Timorous should learn to be more expressive and selfless, thinking equally of others as he thinks of himself.

CAUSTIC-SERVICE CHAMELEON

Some of the outstanding factors of the Caustic are his unwavering strength, sternness, ability to create a course, a goal and follow through irrespective of people's opinion. The service chameleon on the other hand tries to please people and be among the winning group. His primary desire lies with what other personnel perceive of him and him aligning himself by being like the very best. The combination of the caustic – service chameleon is a soldier who follows stern policies, tries to be a leader that does not display weakness, but in the overall will waver in his policies, divert from his course or goal to appease a greater audience. Apart from their rigidity or stern policies, they love to be appreciated, loved by others and for personnel to say good things about them generally. They are ready to compromise whatever goal to suit those needs. They make good leaders and are disciplined as soldiers. They live their lives to reflect against everything they detest in the service. If it is illiteracy for instance, they ensure there are educated, that their spouses are educated, as well as their children. They try very hard not to borrow or live on credit. While they try to live up to these expectations, they boast about them and use them as examples at every opportunity. Moreover, whenever they do this, they normally do it in a way that looks down on others. They might not be sensitive enough to understand this but their audience does and whenever they fall short of their words, others will not hesitate to use their very words against them. The Caustic- service – Chameleon is a good soldier with a heart towards others and their needs, but still suffers the emotional fluctuations which the basic Caustic suffers in expression of anger, love, and hatred etc.

CONCEIT-CAUSTIC

The Conceit-Caustic on first appearance might seem an introvert, because they find it difficult to blend or attach easily. However, once they are in their comfort zones, they are more extroverted. As a soldier, rating, or aircraftman, the Conceit- Caustic is the most organized and intelligent among the groups. Basically, a conceit has good looks or averagely they stand out. But to the Conceit-Caustic, their looks and physicality do not really meet up to their expectation. Moreover, having in one way or the other experienced challenges of service personnel, they have formed personal theory about the other ranks' cadre, especially the aspects they dislike and have always criticized, which have in the past affected their personal lives negatively. Some may term the military discipline to be dwindling and not as it is supposed to be. An observation they have acquired as Conceits having grown up in barracks, attended military schools or something in that relation. Some may want to believe that the order ranks' cadre can outshine officers' cadre both intellectually and financially. Some of their theories can be against the injustice of officers to the order ranks or exploitation, the list goes on and on. Now these theories are not just formed on a one-day basis, but rather a trend that is picked up before they joined the service. As soon as they joined the service, the Caustic side of them begins to manifest. If the Conceit-Caustic has a vendetta against officers' exploitation or injustice, he does not just sit and complain. They make sure that this trend does not affect them and if occurrence of such becomes a scene, they are not afraid to confront an officer openly about the wrong. When they do, they are mostly termed to be right and are backed up by laws. For the Conceit-Caustic who believes discipline is dwindling, always get familiar with military laws and codes. You do not want to get in the way of this one especially if he is a provost. "They always carry the job for head" They sing discipline, live discipline and eat discipline even at their own detriment. In essence, what I try to elucidate is that the conceit part of this person makes him organized, reasonable, understanding, social and interactive. The caustic part gives him a cause to follow and the zeal and persistence to push on. The Conceit-Caustic is organized and his course is obvious but he is not without flaws. His major flaws come from his caustic side and sometimes push them too far. This type hardly have real friends, their ideology, paranoia and all they need to do to fulfill their course push people away from them. Although they yearn for friendship and companionship they have lost track on how to get it. The Conceit-Caustic appears to be rational, expecting that everything be done in order and accordingly; that is with respect to their lives and everything that surrounds them.

The extent they go to maintain their assumed position, to continue the course takes a great toll on them financially, physically, psychologically, spiritually and emotionally and in all ramifications of life. What makes it worse is they do not know when to stop their ideologies and the course they have established, because it is now their way of life even above their families. What they do is to rationalize it to themselves that they are actually on the right track and people around get confused about the capacity of their innate nature that seems rather unstable and volatile. However deep inside, they know they have lost their way but are just too proud or rigid to admit and make things right. The Conceit-Caustic is an excellent blend that if developed well and managed properly will make an excellent leader and a good friend. What this type truly needs is proper understanding of what are truly important. These are the love of God, the family and inter-personal relationship. They are also to deal with their pride, face and admit their mistakes squarely irrespective of their words of discipline, what tenet their course may hold or what people will say. They are to learn that to make a mistake or to admit a wrong is not a sign of weakness but rather a sign of strength.

CONCEIT-SERVICE CHAMELEON

These types are poster soldiers, uniform starched, ironed and sparkling boots, basically no sky lacking. When you see them you will love the armed forces. They are punctual to work and to an average level, they know their duties, and when off duties they have the best wardrobe ever. They are dandies and the women generally love them. When you enter their house you just fall in love, it has everything, the latest electronic and gadgets, the most recent ones, ranging from Air-conditioner to Television just mention it they seem to have a perfect life. In addition, they are smart, with a good command of English, and have great style. In a ship, unit or establishment when a senior officer needs a new orderly, they are usually first pick. But when they get closer to the officer concerned, he gets irritated by what their lives truly are, "a façade". How they lie to keep face and their need for everyone to adore them at all times are exposed when one gets close to them. The conceited-service chameleon is a people's person; more of a sanguine who laughs and plays his way around but also takes pleasure in leading a perfect life for the world to see. They are very lazy and will grumble all they can, in face of work especially what they consider dirty jobs which they have sworn never to do but the service keeps throwing it in their face. They do not have very serious lives and most of their plans are based on the present and not the future, and at the end of the day, most of them suffer because they cannot meet up the life they profess. Most times people in this blend are always lucky and things just turn-out to favor them. As leaders, they struggle to succeed because seriousness is not a word for them and if they seem to be, it means their ego is on the line.

Another major flaw of the conceit-service chameleon is his ego and the need to be adored and courted by others. If this soldier will just believe in himself and put aside what people will say or think about him, his success will be tremendous. Since the service itself generally loves him and because of his output he gets rare opportunities, like abroad course or orderly with important senior officers et cetera. Nevertheless, the need to keep face kills him more than anything does. He needs to understand that the world and its attributes are all vanity upon vanity, to embrace humility knowing that pride goes before a fall. In addition, if he is able to be confident in his output, no matter what people think about him, he will truly succeed and be a better person.

CONCEIT-EUPHORIC

This blend are the most slow to learn among the conceit blends. However, one smart choice they make is in choosing acquaintances. They always tend to befriend responsible and disciplined people who would point them to the right direction when they are erring in their ways. They generally possess the basic qualities of every conceit and are neat and sharp to work. They avoid trouble and amongst the conceit group, the conceit-euphoric is the coolest and most loyal. They are very generous especially to whichever soldier that is their close acquaintance. Their extravagance is also on the extreme. Although they do not live superfluous lives, they take great pleasure in socializing and do not do it alone. And though it cost them much, it never bothers them. Whenever they socialize and spend, they want other soldiers to witness and talk about it in either the barracks or their units, on how they spend on drinks and in bars carrying everybody along irrespective of the cost. They virtually drink every day or socialize, as far as there is money to take the team with them. Likewise, if they cannot take the team, they cling to the closest of their acquaintance who is of course a disciplined person. Therefore, if he drinks, he drinks responsibly that is why as much as he socializes he hardly gets into trouble at work. When it comes to bragging, they normally take the front seat. Unlike the conceit-service chameleon who wants his so-called perfect life to be seen and adored, the conceit-euphoric tends to brag about everything. They are admirable storytellers and when they are not fearful, they make good soldiers especially while on operations. As leaders, either as a CBM, RSM or CSM on their own they do not turn out to be good leaders so they always have a back-ground man, an intelligent or clever adviser that directs their steps. The conceit-euphoric has to look inward and evaluate himself. He needs to discover what he is really good at and go after it on his own. This type will make good soldiers if only they can understand that those days they lived as barracks' boys, EX- boys or a related scenario are quite different from their adulthood. Like I have written before, most conceit lived in, or grew up close to a military barracks or are EX- boys. So naturally, the conceit-euphoric has to understand that to be a good soldier you must not be smart, intellectual or praised for debauchery. Rather, set your heart to serve and pursue the course, which you know you can achieve.

CONCEIT-AUSTERE

Let us view this blend first from the angle of his family and acquaintances. If he is married, his home is run like a military base and if not his girlfriend or lover is treated like a military subordinate. Of all the bends, this type is the strictest. Their thirst for justice is on the superfluous especially when they have a spiritual or moral inclination. It is only natural for the Austere to have outside business interest, but for this blend of austere, that trend is absent. What is represented here is a frugal and stern person that takes value in every penny that emanates from his pockets; they are overly frugal even to themselves. When it comes to military discipline and turnout, they rate above average. They respect their seniors, are punctual to work, parades, and tend to form a good working relationship with those around them. Conversely, they will not hesitate to usurp the authority of a gullible superior. Superiors that are slow to action naturally irritate them. In explaining the Conceit-Austere it should be understood that the line between morality/spiritually and the absence of that affects greatly their psychological expression. For instance, a morally inclined Conceit- Austere will dedicate his being to the embellishment of the moral standard he upholds and it will be reflected in his character at work. He will frown at bribes, laxity and any form of embezzlement. He will be a pillar of discipline even if enforcing it will be at his own detriment he will forge ahead. His home and family are not left out too; he instills the same standard. As a leader CBM or RSM, he will stand up against a corrupt officer and so long as you are not off track with his idealism of morality, he will support your course and fight for it. On the other hand, conceit-austere that is not morally or spiritually inclined loves money, pleasure, materialistic things, and especially when it is given free. They hate to spend their pay on such things, so they are prone to accept gifts as bribes, promote embezzlement, and corrupt practices. As a leader whether CBM or RSM, and an officer is embezzling the money of his men, the only reason he will stand up to the officer is if his cut is not paid to him. However, once he is appeased, he will look the other way. The line between morality and its vice is a thin one. The extent of the greed of the Conceit-Austere is a strong one that in cutting that line only a spiritual inclination can hold him still. On a general note, the conceit-austere is a good and capable leader that sees the end from the beginning; with the proper balance of morality he will be the best he can be.

CONCEIT-TIMOROUS

A sentence to describe this type is "A good and dedicated friend". If there is one thing they understand, it is friendship, but typically with a select few and mostly conceits. Wherever they serve, as soldiers, ratings or aircraftmen, they are loved and accepted because they can be gentle, self-sacrificing, organized, neat, and always punctual to work. They would not disobey any order on purpose or go against authority except if they are pushed. Besides, even if they are pushed, they complain and by the time they finally explode, people tend to understand their issues and offer them both moral support and physical backing. The conceit part of them is a source of pride and egotism, but the timorous part of them subdues this trend to a high level making them display humility unlike the average conceit. At times, they will carry out menial errands that an average conceit will grumble over or even disagree to carry out. Whereas at the same time it becomes very open to sense that the errands are not just undertaken by them as a result of timidity or gullibility but a matter of choice which at any time they can voice their objections. Of all the conceit blends, they have the highest number of acquaintances, and women are naturally glued to them, most times not for sexual purposes but they tend to exhibit a kind of calm that the women feel at liberty to stay under. As family men, they have excellent family setting. They support and love their wives, and their children lack nothing; such are their devotion to family. Money is hardly a priority for them so they do not fight or lobby to go on operations, or operational bases. They allow it to come naturally, and if it will be detrimental to their family course, they will avoid it. The conceit-timorous is not without a set of weakness. They may seem loyal and are admired by many and most times officers and senior officers like to take them as god-sons and at intervals use them. Officers hardly see them as people that should be over-used; such is the luck they draw; their charisma naturally draws them luck. Nevertheless, amidst all these lies an emotional meter that cannot be manage by the Conceit-Timorous himself. His emotional gauge has no control; it fluctuates and is sometimes uncontrollable. When he slides into depression, he can be very irritating and hard to get to; and if it is not checked, might turn to a powerful explosion that will surprise all. Most times, it is during this explosion that they say their mind. They find it difficult to complain when an acquaintance asks a favor of them. Instead they agree and complain to anyone close by and until it builds up, they hardly air out their mind until it turns to a grudge then something else. The Conceit- Timorous knows how to be a good friend and to sacrifice to that effect. However, what he truly needs is to know when to draw the line as to the extent of friendship and the sacrifices he makes in respect of this. Also he needs to know how many friends he wants to keep and to what extent he will sacrifice for a friend. Next is to deal with his fear and emotional swings by having faith in God and understanding that everybody cannot be like them; that people are of different kinds and of different characters, rather he should trust in God to direct his ways.

EUPHORIC-CAUSTIC

He is a debtor; people are always after him when salary is paid. That is why you hardly see him after payment until he has finished spending his money; he resurfaces again both in his office and in his debt joint. He drinks and embarrasses himself, falling into gutters, sometimes you see people embarrassing him concerning his debt. The extremes of this blend always have the welfare office splitting their salaries for their wives and children and giving them just tokens to take care of their alcoholic needs. He applies for loan whenever he can access it without his family's knowledge, and end up going home with barely 30% or 40% of the amount he takes as loan. He first gets to his regular spot, impresses them there, and goes home with whatever that is left. It is when the deduction is effected on his salary that his family would get to know. As a soldier, rating, or aircraftman, he is untamable, and he is a best friend to the RSM or CBM, because he is blunt, and when he is drunk, it becomes worse. Irrespective of your rank or position, he will tell you to your face your wrongs and he may seem right. He only comes to work when he likes, and his superiors just ignore him. He seems smart and intelligent, and these show in his utterances especially when drunk. He spends his time in whore houses and bars. Hidden flaws come again in the fact that, this type can easily impregnate a girl from outside compounding his issues. The Euphoric-Caustic gets his promotions most times and manages to stay afloat through his life in service, but has no investment or anything in that relation as a landmark. If at all he has anything, he must have gotten them in the days before he discovered the joy of getting drunk or the sweetness of women.

People take pity on them but they do not pity themselves. This attitude gives their children complex in school and in their environment generally. Some of them married from joint and club houses, and as such, they may not have decent wives. They are always quarreling and fighting each other and this goes a long way in affecting their children psychologically. More often than not, the military command normally overlooks this trend; but I will strongly recommend rehabilitation and counseling.

EUPHORIC-REPRESSED

This blend is worse than the euphoric-caustic and you cannot afford to punish them, for the fear that they could drop down. They are always unkempt both in and outside the uniform. His welfare is not his business; his only business is to drink and forget his problems. He has many family issues; his best way of handling them is to take alcohol. A lot of them are dismissed because they are always at the wrong place, at the wrong time without the right words to set them free. Some others get missing or die mysteriously and others retire, without getting the due promotion.

He has a pathetic life both in and out of service. This group most times, after retirement, the family does not get to live with them; they just abandon them and move ahead as they are of no use to their families.

EUPHORIC-SERVICE CHAMELEON

All Euphoric blends share one thing in common and that is drinking and whoring, spending time in bars and night in whorehouses. Euphoric Service-Chameleon is no different, he drinks to stupor and he is often carried home smelling, ricking of Alcohol. He never attends to the needs of his family and his Commanding Officer or the barracks officer is always settling their cases. This type retires after 35 years' service as, at most, sergeant and its equivalent. Most of them can spend over twenty years as Able Seamen and in the army they can go decades without promotion and remain as private soldiers. Their service documents are filled with charges and different cases. Their lives are messed up and their bodies weakened and paled because of the kind of spirit they drink without any care. When you see them, you cannot but just have pity on their lives and the effect and toll it takes on their families. As I suggested earlier, a military rehabilitation center should be established to tend their case. Although in their docile state, they may seem humble and interesting, but that docility does not last too long before they start drinking again. The major difference between a Euphoric-Service-Chameleon and Euphoric Timorous/Repressed is that the Euphoric-Timorous / Repressed normally does not combine their drinking habit with whoring. While the other drinks out rightly without controlling its consequences on both themselves and their families.

EUPHORIC-CONCEIT

The Euphoric-Conceit, I can say is the blend that got the better deal in all the euphoric blends and that is because of their conceited nature. Conceit attracts conceits; they are proud and egocentric, confident and most times lucky. This type has friends that are organized, lovers that mostly point them in the right direction that probably for a week or two they abstain.

The egocentric nature imbedded in their conceited person will not push them to drink to stupor or falling into gutters. These types deal majorly in Indian hemp or other related drugs. They dress neatly both in civil and even when going to work. Although they are master 'Job buyer' (getting into trouble) and are naturally troublemakers, they do have their uses in the service. This blend is also lucky because most offences they commit, the command for one reason or the other just gives them a punishment and overlooks the whole issue, instead of a trial. A unique factor about this blend is the kind of women they attract; good and timid women, who see them and fall in love with their stubbornness and their guts. The women believe deep within them that they can be changed, but by the time the relationship is over they come out hurt and disappointed. Because if he changes this week, next week, he is back to his habit again; on and off and most times they end up never getting married until it becomes almost too late. They can squander their one year's investment in one day. This blend also needs a more pro-longed rehabilitation program; one initiated by the military to suit the needs of a soldier.

REPRESSED-CAUSTIC

The most outstanding factor of the Repressed-Caustic is his sadistic nature. It becomes so vivid because that is what his life is all about most times; haunting his subordinate and making them pay dearly for what in a normal day can be overlooked. In describing both the Repressed and Caustic, I emphasized that the Caustic, during his childhood must have had a course, something he felt was wrong and he could not stop, but bore it throughout his days of growing-up. That has come to become a major landmark in his ideology. While the Repressed on the other hand was denied many things he ought to have been privy to, hence making him lacking/wanting and feeling empty when he recounts his ordeal as a child. His struggle as a man before he joined the service becomes something he brings into the military service, blaming everybody that is not like him for his assumed predicament. He does not come out to the street to shout it out, but it is present in his actions. His response when his subordinate is found wanting by him and his words in the background attest to this. When his subordinates talk about him, they call him sadist, and when his superiors ponder him, they see a viper. These types are rare but when you meet them, you will want to give them their space. The average Caustic, as a judge or leader   listens to reasons and acts accordingly but this blend acts out of sheer wickedness. From a neutral point of view, I have tried to view what good is to be sought of this blend. I then remembered again that they are excellent carriers of bad news. It pleases them to spread and gloat on it. They take pleasure in the dismissal of soldiers who have put everything on the line to serve their country. Their mind has been altered and the only route of renewal is to accept Allah, to accept Jesus Christ and embrace a spiritual life with devotion. Many personnel in this blend who were saved have found their answers in the Bible and Quran and are living a just life. If you are one, do not mind my harsh word and do not dismiss it, " Saying" This is rubbish"; calm down accept yourself for who you are and embrace God. He is the only way.

REPRESSED- TIMOROUS

The timorous-Repressed is what I call a better soldier. His tendency towards the cunning nature of the Repressed group is reduced to the barest minimum by the under laying Timorous trait. By nature, he is a traditionalist that does not take much pleasure in the conventional. As per turn out he rates averagely and is relatively disciplined at work. He is quiet, keeps to himself, and does not speak out of turn, instead will lash out against some who do. The combination of Repressed-Timorous has a tendency towards mediocrity and as leaders they tend to express it, blaming faults on higher authority even though they can initiate changes. They can express a level of sternness, which might be unexpected most times due to their timid nature. This blend is not prone to sociality; they do not have a knack for it, they are prudent spenders as they put much effort in giving their families a good life. I cannot say they are perfect but they are kind of in-between. They do not possess great ambition to do outstanding things or become officers, if it comes they take it, at the same time, on their own level they tend to do well. On the other hand, when you seek a third opinion on their person you normally do not get a good response. Their public relation is very poor and when they try to make it look good, they just make it worse. In conclusion, the Repressed- Timorous already has all he needs to be the best. What he majorly needs is to realize that the life of a soldier is mostly open and that word spreads, making it easy for an observer to learn about our innate nature. First, he must accept himself for who he is and be able to defend his flaws and the side effects of his actions and inactions. He must understand that only his word alone and excuses cannot build his person or change people's opinion. Moving selfishly and solely in life is not the answer and cannot keep them from trouble if it wants to come. They should understand that the life of a soldier must be lived in unison with both superior and subordinates.

REPRESSED-SERVICE CHAMELEON

One exceptional factor about the Repressed is their ability to observe from a distance without being in the center of event. Most times, when they do, the resulting information they get from their observation is not used for their betterment but just stored somewhere in their long-term memory. With the combination of the Service-Chameleon as a blend, the information is not just stored but it is actually applied. Now the Repressed has a tendency towards being in the background, while his Service-Chameleon blend has a tendency towards watch, learn and reflect. These types are master copycat, but what differentiates them from the primary Service-Chameleon is that they copy word for word, action for action. A normal Service-Chameleon will alter what he learns when he decides to reflect. The Repressed Service-Chameleon does not have the luxury of that. He watches the best, observes the best and does exactly what the best does. Going as far as dressing like them, using their exact same words, the list goes on. It is not as if he will not like to alter it to appear more subtle, but he just cannot. His Repressed nature will not allow it, he does not have that much confidence in his own ability to alter it and presents in himself a more formidable character, like the character he imposes. Ordinarily, without someone to look up to, these types are a mess, truthfully they are disorganized, indiscipline, always 'buying jobs'. Whenever it is mentioned of cases against military discipline, they are used as examples. Their life's meter has no gauge; they tend to fluctuate as the trends permits. Today they are overly social; tomorrow they are overly religious, and the next they are in to fashion and so on... When it becomes too cumbersome, they quickly find someone to imitate and they normally pick out the best and the leading team probably in the command they serve or at their residence in the barracks. They imitate and even become better than the persons they choose to impose at most times.

In conclusion, the life of the Repressed-Service-Chameleon in the end is determined by an outstanding figure in his command or residence. Moreover, even when he is posted, he continues to imbibe that nature until he finds a replacement. However, on his own, depending on his own wit and charm, he has come to believe he is a failure in the making. The answer therefore, lies in the ultimate understanding that you can never be who you want to be or who you ought to be by imitating others.

REPRESSED-EUPHORIC

The Repressed-Euphoric, combines the sly nature of the Repressed personality, and the socialistic nature of the Euphoric. These types watch from the background, they do not put themselves at the forefront of events or activities. They obey orders and carry out commands no matter how menial it is. The worst they do is grumble to themselves. Even when they grumble to others, the other party must have initiated the topic. They are naturally introverted, but the euphoric nature imbedded in them tends to make them as extrovert. They love drinking houses, but do not drink to stupor. They love women but will not expend themselves at the expense of their family. To a minimal level, they support their family as they see fit. They always try to blend socially but their petty nature does not allow for that. They love cheap things and mostly when they drink, they prefer to drink cheap spirit that will intoxicate quicker than a beer of equal price. The general nature of the Euphoric is drunkenness and whoring, but the primary presence of the Repressed personality overwhelms that, creating a balance, thus making the Repressed-Euphoric a little organized. He is not as a rule neat but his turn out does not draw so much attention. As a leader, he does not do so well. He makes decisions in haste and out of impulse and blames the faults on his subordinates which do not earn him respect. His social life is a thing of debacle and he is much criticized for that because at times, it interferes with his job and he does not have the discipline to draw a line between his social life and his duties. Taming the way he socializes is a first step to the creation of a better Repressed-Euphoric. In most cases, these types possess intelligence that is below average. Although it is not a leading factor in presenting a better person in them, but when they have good and God-fearing spouses that are probably educated and well learned, it will help them tame this vice at an early stage. I have observed that in the life of a soldier, the spouse is an important factor. The Repressed has a history that is not much of a happy memory when pondered. His family issues, both extended and immediate, work issues make them careful and prudent in their life as a whole. Conversely, given the imbedded euphoric nature and any failure by the Repressed personality to tame its indiscipline, only compounds issues for the Repressed-Euphoric. When that happens and he feels powerless against it, he tends to take his problems to the bar. Drinking always in an effort to forget or not be confronted with the issues he has. However, when he has a spouse of that liking close by, to point him in the right direction, he gains a better understanding of his purpose and becomes a better person. In absence of a spouse that fits my description; a close mentor should suffice.

REPRESSED-AUSTERE

Of the entire repressed blend, the Repressed-Austere is the only one that has embraced himself for whom he is, and is not trying to fit into any social club or imitate any person. This blend understands his prior challenges, his lacks; what he lost growing up, and has made up his mind to give these to his siblings. There is no sociality in his register; his past pains and suffering will never allow such waste. He invests his income and does small business to support his family and plans for retirement. As a leader and when in authority, he takes his time to lecture his subordinates on the harsh reality of life and how one must invest wisely.

He tries to be a father, understanding other's pain and offering moral advice and support where necessary, but he will never sacrifice anything from himself to help others. It is a difficult line most Repressed-Austere do not cross. They can set you on the right path, advise you, but two things stand out. They would not sacrifice for you and they will not want to show you the ways that will allow you to rise above their own status. In all situations, they want to feel comfortably above you. It is what gives them peace and solace; offering advice, tending to people's needs, correcting wrongs but never too much to make a real difference. They prefer giving you fish to taking you to the river and teaching you how to fish. Their comfort zone is you below them and them feeling in control. Lesson for this blend is simple; do not let your place of solace, or comfort abide in the misery and wanting of people, rather let it be placed in their joy and progress, even when their progress extends beyond yours, then will they truly be better soldiers.

SERVICE-CHAMELEON CAUSTIC

The Service-Chameleon Caustic seems stern, resolute frowning on indiscipline and wanting to push his policies. But the distinct thing that is very obvious of the blend is that whatever sternness or resoluteness they possess is not established by their own mind or will, but from information emanating from other sources close to them. Now the Service-Chameleon is a natural copycat, the Caustic is stern and a disciplinarian, creating courses and having enough bile to follow through. As for this blend, they do not have what it takes to see a problem; to see a flaw, to see an opportunity or to calculate possible futures or outcome of an action. But when you present them with a reasonable explanation to an opportunity or a problem that needs solving, they will follow through as if it was their personal course. As for turnout and discipline, they rate average and try to stay in the balance. They talk a lot when they opt to undertake anything; sometimes they talk out their plans until there are no plans left. As Leaders, they want to feel in control; they detest prying eyes, because they are not straightforward. They cheat easily and are full of deceits. Therefore, when they talk most times, you can sense them justifying the deceits that hunt their conscience. A few things stand out about the blend that either has positive or negative effect on them in the long run. They are most times very easy to convince; that with just the right explanation, they can turn sides in an instance. This is because, they do not build a very strong belief or tenets system for themselves and at the same time they like to feel in control, to solve issues and create changes so when they are presented with such; they cannot resist. They have a natural attraction for the opposite sex and live an active social life that seriously affects their retirement plan and the future preparation for their offspring.

In conclusion, the Service-Chameleon-Caustic is better off without a course because he has none of his own. He reflects as a better person in the background carrying out orders and doing his job as he ought to instead of carrying people's burdens without an innate justification or reason.

SERVICE CHAMELEON- AUSTERE

This blend falls under the Aristocrats of the Service. They are the business class who hardly depend on the service pay for their livelihood. The job means little to them. They value it for the little money it puts into their pocket. He socializes on the average, and is not scared of spending money, which is always a calculated spending. He gives for what he gets, and has followers who are interested in his money, and he in turn uses them to achieve his desired goals. He bribes and buys his way through punishment. He sees business opportunity at every unit or establishment he finds himself. Thus, he is a buyer of labor, seller of goods, and a prudent spender. Whenever he spends, it means he has more to gain.

He has a friendly personality; he gets close to people and takes time to study them, not because he is nice or naturally friendly but because he is calculative and has a foresight. He wants to know the powers that run the show, how he can appeal to their conscience and how he can use it to achieve his end and be unstoppable in chasing his money. Everybody notices he is absent on parades and musters, but absentees are sanctioned or punished, but he is not.

The Service-Chameleon-Austere could be a stingy father and husband. This is because when he establishes his wife, he teaches her to be financially independent in order not to interfere with his finance. He has no permanent friend or enemy but permanent interest which he protects with all his heart. Few of this people fall into the order ranks cadre, majority of them are officers.

Most were previously in offices where they have amassed wealth, as ratings, soldiers or aircraftmen. Their business acumen and financial status are irritating to younger officers who are yet to make a landmark in life. As a result, it is not uncommon to see these types befriending senior officers in order to ward off any ill will from what they consider "the little powers". As far as they go, many of these types have lost touch with what it actually takes to be a soldier, because they eventually bribe and intrigue their ways through everything promotion, courses, unwanted posting, operations, you mention it. They are found either in highly sensitive place where they just sit in the office or in an office where their absence will never be noticed. The only major need they require from the service is the identity it gives them. They are not ready to sacrifice anything. As a fellow soldier, you do not want to go to a life or death operation with these types because they will turn tail and run. Their loyalty lies solely in their business enterprise and their bank accounts; any thing standing in the way of this is expendable.

Upon retirement, he lives an excellent average life, but in the real sense he is richer than he actually appears.

SERVICE CHAMELEON-EUPHORIC

This blend is better known as "Mr. Nice guy." They do not have a problem of their own; neither do they need any one to border them with their own problems. All they want to do is go to work, dismount, rest a little, dress up, and party in a drinking joint. Their social life is the most active in their whole out-look. Most times, it gets in the way of their job, so it is common to see them late for parades and musters and when they come late they have a good sense of humor that will see them out of the trouble. In terms of eye service, this blend rates highest. They can do anything to make you smile and just ignore the offence they have committed. They know the right words to use and because of them you just decide to forgive the whole group. But believe me; they will commit the same offence again; because as a rule, they are indiscipline. They cannot do without their usually socializing, that is the only thing that gets in the way between them and their jobs. As leaders, all their policies are created in the bar because as RSM, CBM, or CSM, they have clicks that they carry along so you find them in drinking joints discussing, work issues. The next day, the only thing they are coming to do in the office is sleep, and when they are confronted with heavy decision they re-direct such to their clicks.

On the outside, he seems to have a good relationship with his wife and kids, joking with them and drawing them closer, while in reality, they are the highest sufferers of his indiscipline and immoral actions, which can be either womanizing or drinking. For those of them that have a knack for women, they can have two different wives in different states and still have different mistresses all over. Besides, they are so nice and cunning you will not notice. A very outstanding good about this blend is they are nice and jovial and they try to see the good out of everything. You hardly find female personnel with this blend. One thing this blend lacks at whatever level is discipline. If he has that to an average level he will become the best he can be.

SERVICE CHAMELEON-TIMOROUS

Most of the characteristics of the Service-Chameleon Euphoric can be found in the Service-Chameleon Timorous; but they are some basic distinctions. The Service-Chameleon Timorous is not prone to eye service, in an out ward way; they prefer one on one, because they find it difficult to take sides in public. Their level of discipline is rated higher, so it is rare for their social lives to interfere with their work. As leaders, they are nice jovial and try to carry everybody along. Their own favorite is whom the authority favors. They befriend such personnel and turn them to drinking buddies or chat mates. If he is an RSM, CBM, CSM, or Bofor, when such people commit they overlook their offence and when there is a detail they will not call such favorites even though they are the most junior present. To them, it is their way of showing their loyalty to whichever officer or senior officer that favors those personnel. As junior NCO'S, they gossip a lot. The minute they are with you if you are their superior they praise your work, your idea, your resolution and they discredit whoever they seem to think you dislike or is an active opponent of yours. If you are their junior, they talk about themselves, pointing out the flaw of their immediate seniors and leaders, stressing that they are different and will be more sensitive to the needs of their subordinates. These types can be easily convinced to spy, bribe, loot or anything in that relation. But beware; they will sell to the highest bidder. Those on personal capacities with officers are not relied upon for the big things because it is not too difficult for a keen observes to notice that their loyalty is swerving. The major issue of this blend is their ability to pick sides; to decide fully where to stand in life. It is a peculiar trait with every Service – Chameleon.

TIMOROUS-CONCEIT

One of the major features of the Timorous is his introverted nature; making him a diplomat; reserved in action and of few word. There are two angles to every blend of the timorous; one is when they are as superior over others, in leadership positions as CBM, RSM, Bofor or CSM or when they are still very subordinate as early soldiers. The major and very visible characteristics of his timorous nature are his calmness and diplomacy, understanding and conceding. The distinction appears on the other hand when he is endowed with power at work, or his financial status has risen or he needs to actively stand up to a challenge. Then his conceited part will surface but although on a more subdued note. His ego is not as inflated as the primary conceit, nor is his confidence, but he proves wrong the former idea that he might have been perceived to be; i.e. a mediocre or a gullible man. And when such character surfaces, the immediate change seems to make people see him as a viper. Although the conceit part of him is expressed on a more positive note as in the case of *Timorous- **Caustic***. Where when the caustic nature surfaces, it surfaces as a viper and it actually stings. You will get surprised at what has been hiding beneath the surface. The caustic blends are very insincere with words, disloyal, and above all they can turn and bite their masters. As leaders, they are proud and arrogant and will not take lightly to any subordinate that undermines their authority, either through their action or inaction. The case becomes even worse with the *Timorous **Repressed**.* As lowly servants, sometimes their level of mediocrity irritates you. They are so humble you actually feel embarrassed at their level of humility; because the combination of the repressed trait and the timorous makes them seem lacking both intellectually and in the confidence they reflect. Even people they are superior to comfortably step on them and all they may say in return is... "Please leave them O" "they do not have respect" "I do not want a confrontation". Nonetheless, the moment they gain financial relevance or find themselves in a position of actual power, a side of them comes out, that most never ever contemplated due to their mediocre expressions. Because the gulf between what they were before and what they turn out to become is so great, that is what actually puts people on the edge. Since, that repressed part of them will not listen to reason; It acts selfishly in the interest of himself, and those in the past that thought this blend was their friend are turned off by their action, and even though they try to come close to them, they are repelled either by the Timorous-repressed himself or the character he expresses.

Some Timorous after intensive learning and spiritual enlightenment have learnt to create a bridge between their innate and surface natures, creating a balance in both. The Conceit and Caustic are first to realize the effect of their inhibited nature and work towards it. The Repressed, most times is not smart enough to see it and work on it, and it mostly follows them to their grave; except those with spouses that are ready and dedicated to show them to the right part. In the case of the *Timorous-**Austere*** both personality interact on the same level either as lesser subordinates or as leaders. The

Austere part of them inspires their ambition and helps them stay the course. He acts out his life, expresses himself in all moderate doses among the timorous blends. He is the most motivated. His diplomatic nature allows people to be free and open with him. In most cases, timorous personnel do not push or act on certain information or opportunities that might seem ambitious; the Timorous Austere will pursue it and even while at it he will suppress his ambition and play it out diplomatically. He interacts as he sees fit and his social life is characterized by his objective. He might be a friend but he will not sacrifice or go on the extreme as the average Timorous might do. His associations are based on his objective, so is his way of life. The distinction in this type is that the excesses of the under laying Austere blend is greatly inhibited by the surface Timorous personality, and the tendency towards timidity is regulated by the austere personality.

PART 3

THE TWO SIDES OF EVERY PERSONALITY

In all the seven personalities, there exists no specific one without a set of flaws or difficulties. Their differences vary from one to another. In the military setting, there are certain set of weaknesses that are quite useful in certain operations. At that point, they do not stand as weaknesses but indeed strengths. For instance, a Euphoric that is constantly disregarded for his drinking habit and disciplinary nature can be easily used to gather intelligence. In places where he drinks and smokes, you will be surprised what he can gather. The Caustic in all its sadist nature can be a rigid enforcer where discipline is sensed to be dwindling. The Service-Chameleon as a copycat can adapt to any situation, which is a major factor that makes up the leading soldier. So in analyzing the strength and weakness, we would not outline a table stating strength or weakness. But for every reader, there is an opportunity to discover your personality which is the first step in identifying your shortcomings in every scenario, and how to improve on them.

In further chapters, the basic characteristic of each personality will be tabulated in two tables; for one a clear space would be left for what should be considered a weakness. Like I said earlier, there are certain features that might be considered weaknesses to an everyday man but to a soldier they are needed recipes. The other table will contain what is assumed to be a strength and weakness. In as much as these things vary, it should not serve as an alibi to continue such, because in the overall sense it has no positive effect on the life of the individual. If at any point in time such exigencies are required to aid service operations, it should be short and precise. Now I will go on to analyze the positive attributes of each personality.

AUSTERE: GOOD POINTS

The Austere has a penchant for power, willed either as a command or through the influence of money, he is ambitious and steadfast, possesses enough discipline and determination to see him through his desired goal. The Austere is strategic by nature in his association, expenses and the way he runs his family. He has a good control of his emotion gauge and has learnt to keep it in check. His leadership ability and business acumen add up to make him mostly a successful man upon retirement. He hardly buys on credit before the month's end, whether he has a business or not. It is all dependent on his ability to prioritize and spend based on importance. If he is out socializing, it is a calculated one, which makes him enjoy a cordial relationship with his colleagues. As a soldier, other soldiers virtually borrow from him, in which he will not hesitate to add interest and ensure his payment at month's end. Such is his strategy when money is involved. As a decision maker he wastes no time pondering, he is decisive as he is a realist by nature. The Austere sees the end from the beginning; his ability to visualize the outcome of circumstance makes him stand out and gives him a kind of godlike reference amongst others. They actually reach heights that most other ranks never dare to covet. Most Austere are friends with officers and senior officers, this becomes the way they establish themselves both financially and socially. Some after military service opt into politics. The Austere is truly a success story.

Are you an austere soldier? Take a look at the table below it contains your major attributes. Distinguish what you think are your weaknesses before you continue reading.

The Attributes	What are your weaknesses?
✓ **Business acumen**	
✓ **Clever**	
✓ **Ambitious**	
✓ **Domineering**	
✓ **Firm**	
✓ **Discipline**	
✓ **Neat**	
✓ **Over-achiever**	
✓ **Strategic**	
✓ **Manipulative**	
✓ **Stingy**	
✓ **Leadership qualities**	
✓ **Excessive love for money**	
✓ **Self-reliant**	
✓ **Resolute**	
✓ **Uncompromising**	
✓ **Selfish**	
✓ **Only permanent interest**	
✓ **Unforgiving**	

- ✓ **Quick tempered**
- ✓ **Sociable**
- ✓ **Realist**
- ✓ **Unsympathetic**
- ✓ **Un-Sacrificing**
- ✓ **Lacking in team work**
- ✓ **Usurper**
- ✓ **Cold**
- ✓ **Impetuous**
- ✓ **Fetish**
- ✓ **Impatience**
- ✓ **Revengeful**
- ✓ **Goal-oriented**
- ✓ **decisive**

AUSTERE: THE OTHER SIDE

The drive for success and over-achievement normally, if not always pushes the Austere too far. Among all personalities, the Austere has a high tendency towards fetish things and spiritual consultations. Once an Austere has drawn his road map, he does not care who he destroys along the way, who he endangers, who he drags behind. As long as you do not have any power over him, or cannot stop his progress in his foreseeable future, he would betray you and move on. He has a cold heart whose only love is money and position and would manipulate to get his way. When it comes to teamwork, he does not do so well. His primary concern does not go with the team, and even during military operations, he mostly looks out for himself. Only in rare cases will he offer support but not at his personal bodily harm. The Austere as a person might seem flexible which is relative to the overall achievement of his set goal, but outside that line, he can be rigid and uncompromising. He will not hesitate to take charge of a gullible leader where he serves either directly or indirectly. As a rule, he hates a slow or dull person and would not take lightly of such under his leadership. His patience will burnout and the person will suffer his wrath, which can be inhuman. In the overall sense, the Austere sees everybody as a tool to aid him in reaching his goal. His goal and so-called ambition have been infused into even his family life that there no longer exist a thing called love or harmony. In some cases, he appears to have a stable home on the outside but inwardly his family yearns for what is supposed to be of an actual family.

Now you have seen the negatives, let's reanalyze the weaknesses based on what you have written down before. These are what I think are your strength and your weakness, based on the practicality of what has just been explained.

Austere- Strength	Austere- Weakness
Business acumen	Selfish
Clever	Manipulative
Ambitious	Disloyal(only permanent interest)
Domineering	Unforgiving
firm	Un sacrificing
Discipline	Lacking in specialization
Neat	Usurper
Strategic	domineering
Leadership ability	Fetish
Self – Reliant	Impatience
Resolute	Revengeful
Quick tempered	Excessive love for money
Outgoing	Uncompromising
Realist.	Over achiever
Goal-Oriented	Cold
Decisive	Impetuous

CAUSTIC: THE GOOD POINTS

The Caustic soldier is a visionary, whose visions do not necessarily have to be rewarding financially or otherwise. He is a crusader who would sacrifice almost anything to see his course fulfilled. His zeal and support for authoritarian will, irrespective of what is perceived of the authority by the lesser soldier makes him more than efficient in carrying out his orders. He more than certainly will not add emotions to his workload. He is a researcher whether he has the brain or not, i.e. finds his way around any puzzle that he needs answers to in relations to his desired course. He always has a course; a course with a power source, fueled by either his past, or a present that alters the past, putting to naught what he believes in. In face of challenges, he is a witted talker combing facts with details. He is a lover of both political and religious debates, as far as they have higher relevance. He tries to be skilled in his specialization especially if it involves his course, then he will be the best in it. He is a stern soldier with enough fuel to confront any challenge or opposition to what he perceives is right. It is only a Caustic soldier that will stand up to a General, not to undermine his authority, but to prove himself right in showing the General the wrong of his way. In face of his sternness, he is a compromising soldier who would listen to reason when reasoned with.

Caustic – The Attributes	What are your weaknesses?
Supporter of authority	
Twisted past	
Discipline with work	
Intellectual	
Rational / Reasonable	
Social loners	
Researcher	
Witted- talker	
Love debate	
Activist	
Insensitive	
Efficient	
Rigid	
Anxious	
Visionary	
Aggressive enforcer	
Weak- conscience	

Paranoid

Indiscipline in personal lives

Critical

Negative

Extremist

Pretender

Self-centered

Unfriendly

Sarcastic

Emotional

Idealist

Stern

Skilled in specialization

Very forward

Job buyer(getting into troubles)

Hot tempered

Resolute

Pessimistic

Harbors resentment

Spreader of bad news

Frustrated

Persecutor

CAUSTIC: THE OTHER SIDE

The Caustic is the least loved soldier among his subordinates and even his superiors. His aggressive way of enforcing orders and cruel nature serve as source of concern to even the authority. His self-perceived lack of good looks, twisted past and paranoia make him criticize and see the negative out of almost anything. His character that pushes people away makes him easily suspicious of others. He preaches discipline but on his own terms once he is alone he is indiscipline. His family members are aware of this also and do not respect him. When he socializes, he can be an extremist withdrawing into his shell after he has over exhausted himself and pretends about it. He is self-centered and loves to take advantage of other people. He harbors resentment and he is, as a rule, vengeful. He finds pleasure in gloating on other people's mishaps and bad news generally. He has a caustic/sarcastic tongue that could break a fragile heart. His hot temper and over forwardness makes him a Job buyer (getting into trouble). His past determines his course, and his shortcomings are the very things he wages war against, and persecutes in other people, but not himself; loosing himself and what is relevant in the process.

A tough read I must confess; what then are your weaknesses in relation to what you selected earlier; here is my table of your probable strength and weakness.

Caustic- Strength	Caustic- Weakness
Discipline with work	Aggressive enforcer
Supporter of authority	Paranoid
Intellectual	Indiscipline in personal lives
Rational / Reasonable	Critical
Researcher	Extremist
Witted- talker	Self-centered
Love debate	Unfriendly
Activist	Sarcastic
Efficient	Harbor resentment
Visionary	Spreader of bad news
Resolute	Revengeful
Skilled in specialization	Persecutor
Strong- willed	Hot- tempered
Stern	Very forward

CONCEIT: THE GOOD POINTS

The Conceit is naturally admired by other personalities. He has a keen understanding of the military ways even before enlistment.

He is good looking and young, smart and most times intelligent. He has a natural attraction for the military job, and he is the type that would first call it... "My father's job" He is an optimistic soldier with a good sense of humor that understands human suffering. By nature, the Conceits are neat and dress sharpest to work; they are organized and independent minded soldiers, who show intuitive and have the best command voice, with adequate knowledge in their specialization. As leaders, they can delegate responsibilities; they hate illegalities and try as much as possible to be perfectionists in what they reflect and would expect it from colleagues and friends. He is an enthusiastic soldier; the least depressed in all the personality types, compassionate and lively. People generally like to socialize with him because he knows how to catch fun and is quite enjoyable. They are also proud and confident in their status no matter how inferior it is. The Conceit is a loyal soldier who believes in service integrity.

Is that who you truly are? Then fill out your weakness!

The Conceit- Attributes	What are your weakness
Good looks	
Young	
Brags	
Egocentric	
Loves the spotlight	
Love for the military	
Optimistic	
Narcissist	
Hates obligations	
Perfectionist	
Extravagance	
Sense of humor	
Organized	
Independent minded	
Intuitive	
Confidence	
Sharp talkers	
Avoids risk	

Loyal

Service integrity

Touchy

Lucky

Materialistic

Delegators

Enthusiastic

Stubborn

Outgoing

sociable

sharp dresser

CONCEIT: THE OTHER SIDE

If you are drawn to him today and tomorrow, then the next he begins to irritate you. The Conceits are touchy, self-protective and mostly emotional. They tend to avoid risks and are particular about the kind of friends they keep. They prefer friends who are social, wasteful, and extravagant like them. As egocentric as they are, they would prefer someone who would guard that part. This is because they would not want their personal lives to be a public debate. Their wasteful and extravagant nature makes them braggers with a sweet tongue to complement it. They live above their means and pursue things that are bigger than they are, and in all they do, they like the spotlight, to be admired and talked about, for how their lives are perfect and different from the conventional soldiers. At work, the Conceits hate obligation, and are often lazy; they would not mind to pay off people/other soldiers to carry out certain duties they feel too big to do.

All these excessive nature of his make his life too cumbersome to bear and he keeps getting into it deeper by the day. It has become his way of life even until retirement. It is a good thing to be aware of one's weakness, because that is the first step to defeating it completely. Here is a list of what I think are your strengths and weaknesses.

Conceit- Strengths	Conceit- Weakness
	Narcissists
Compassionate	Brags
Young	Hates obligation
Love for the military	Lazy
Optimistic	Wasteful
Good sense of humor	Egocentric
Sharp dresser	Heightened socialization
Independent minded	
Intuitive talkers	Exaggerates
Self- confidence	Touchy
Delegators	Avoids risk
Hate illegalities	Loves the spotlight
Sociable	Extravagant
Loyal	Stubborn
Service integrity	Materialistic

EUPHORIC: THE GOOD POINTS

A philosophy states, that what really matters is what you perceive of yourself. It is what you say it is. To the Euphoric, no matter people's opinion of him, he is enjoying life and drinking away his sorrows and all that matter that indeed make him happy and he reflects that happiness because his talks are quite funny. It helps elevate the mind through laughing. The man hardly judges anyone; he takes it as it comes. The service has leant to tolerate him and punishes him minimally for his many offences.

Euphoric-Attributes	What are your weakness
Make people laugh	
Job buyer(getting into trouble)	
Drunks	
Debtors	
Indiscipline	
Propensity for hawkers	
Issues with authority	
Family problems	
Rarely sober	
Self-justification	
Live in the present	
No vision	
Hardly judge	
Speak out of turn	
Source of concern	
Physically feeble	
Victims of service exigencies	
Always in cell	
Talkative	
Children are back ward	

Most likely to marry a hawker

Die mysteriously

Dirty and unkempt

Jovial

The service tolerates them

Short distinct goals

No promotions

Trouble makers

Always happy

EUPHORIC: THE OTHER SIDE

The Euphoric is the most popular onboard in his ship or establishment. Days after his resumption, everybody knows him, because of the rate at which he 'buys job' and the personnel he has approached to borrow money from. He always has an issue of debt. He has a high propensity for women, and can go as far as having sex with a hawker on credit, and sometimes some of them end up with some of these women as their wives. His personal issues with the authority, his family problems, his disciplinable nature and lack of vision are too hard to handle that they hardly stay sober, always drinking. He lives in the present moment and has justified all his action to himself, which is what matters to him; not what others perceive of him. He is prone to speaking out of turn; his physical feebleness, dwindling health and constant cases are sources of concern to all. He is no visitor to the guardroom due to his 'job buying (getting into trouble)' and troubles making coupled with his dirty and unkempt nature deter his promotions. In most cases, they die mysteriously because they have no inhibition as to where they enter or how long they stay out and who they offend once they are drunk. His family members suffer the most for his euphoric nature.

Euphoric- Strength	Euphoric- Weakness
Make people laugh	Job buyer(getting into trouble)s
The service tolerates them	Always drunk
Talkative	Debtors
Charted a short distinct goals	Indiscipline
Justified in their action	Propensity for hawkers
Always happy	Family problems
Hardly judge	live in the present
	No vision
	Physically feeble
	Victims of service exigencies
	frequently in cell
	Marry wrongly
	Mysterious death
	Dirty and unkempt
	No promotion
	Trouble makers

REPRESSED: THE GOOD POINTS

One of the many things that affect the average soldiers is their lack of proper spending; once salary is paid within one to two weeks, it has all been expended. In the case of the Repressed, he might not have business acumen and the ambition to pursue big positions and dreams, but he is a realist of life's problems and circumstances.   And he has come to accept it the way it is, putting aside pride or anything in that regard. When it comes to prudent spending, the Repressed is excellent in this and will stoop as low as possible when ordered, even if the order sometimes might appear to be unlawful. He hates a life of waste and is himself a disciplined soldier who would do anything to prevent a charge to be brought up against him. This characteristic of his makes him admired by officers because his humility is not something psychological or genetic, but a reality he has come to accept. Given his nature, most times, it is difficult for him to concentrate during innovation but even with this, the Repressed has an open mind that is ready to learn even if it is coming from his junior.

Repressed- Attributes	What are your weaknesses?
Value the Service	
Humble	
Hate waste	
Petty	
Mostly over-aged on entry	
Childhood characterized by Struggle/ostracization	
Mediocre	
Disorganized	
Rough and Unkempt	
Sly	
Unreliable with words	
Switch Sides easily	
Traditional	
Realistic about life	
Disciplined	
Unreasonable	
Unstable	
Slow to learn	
Shrouds personal ambition	

Bad leaders

Ready to learn

Always grumble in the back ground

Confusion during parades

Has a lot of family problems

Difficulty concentrating

Easily offended

Cunning

Industrious

REPRESSED: THE OTHER SIDE

The Repressed expressions are somewhat influenced by circumstances in his past that presented into the future which he is experiencing now. His humility stems from the fact that he has developed a mediocre mind from an influence in the past; it is not a fact that he is humble by nature. His realism is catalyzed by his former struggles; his major actions are dependent on a long-term experience. That can be firm at times but sometimes not strong enough to determine his action. This is why the Repressed can be termed unstable, because his own innate nature has been subdued by something else. This factor is what has cropped up the majority of the negatives attracted to this personality. He has a sly nature and always wants to belong among the social elites, to be able to disobey an order and get away with it, like a Conceit or Service Chameleon would most times. Nobody has more family problems like the Repressed; he has so many challenges so his mind is always wondering, the result of this is him not doing well at work, lagging behind and getting punished for petty instructions he fails to assimilate. The Repressed tend to see everything from the angle of his own suffering taking it out at times on innocent soldiers. As a leader, he can be so unreasonable; he punishes without mercy and will not feel a thing because to him, it is just a part of life.

Review your strength and weakness;

Repressed- Strength	Repressed- Weakness
Value their job	Mediocre
Hate waste	Mostly married with children before joining
prudent	
Realistic about life	Bad turnout
Discipline	Unreliable with words
Appreciated by officers	Lacks Loyalty
Ready to learn	Impractical
Industrious	Unstable mind
	Slow to learn

SERVICE CHAMELEON: THE GOOD POINTS

One of the leading characters of a good soldier is the ability to adapt to circumstances without allowing it to affect your output. The Service Chameleon is a natural adapter and upon this, he is always skilled in his specialization, his shrewd observing skills result in a sub-conscious impulse to always be in league with the winning team. As a follower he does well, showing loyalty to the leaders on top. As a rule, he is people's person; nice, interactive and even-tempered which gives others the desire to trust him easily. In the service proper, the Service-Chameleon seems to excel in his career. Whether or not he is a copycat, the end result justifies the means for him which in most cases is a financially stable retirement.

Service Attributes	Chameleon-	What are your weakness
Natural adapter		
Excellent copy cat		
Skilled in specialization		
Sociable		
High affinity for crime		
Shrewd observers		
Loves high-service		
Good with cover ups		
Disloyal		
Good soldiers		
Good followers		
Compromising		
Care free		
Even tempered		
Jovial		
Easily discouraged		
Excel in career		
Bad leaders		
Talkative		
Easily trusted		
Pleasant nature		

SERVICE-CHAMELEONS: THE OTHER SIDE

A soldier as flexible as the Service-Chameleon is tantamount to disloyalty, switching sides in accordance to your score-board. It is no longer news that he is unprincipled because on his own he has created none. All the principles he currently lives by are trumpeted up from years of imitating others. All these make the Service–Chameleon very prone to betrayal and a chameleon indeed; because he can become easily discouraged. He never has enough will to stay the course. As a leader, his weakness becomes more than visible. He becomes too scared of decisions that will be solely his responsibility. Instead, he will make reference to former leaders and behave exactly how they would have behaved or how they handle similar situations in the past. He is prone to be a traditionalist following what is laid instead of finding his own path and when it fails, he quickly blames others. He never accepts himself for who he is, that is his biggest weakness.

Service Chameleon-strength	Service Chameleon-weakness
Natural adapter	Love high service
Skilled in specialization	High affinity for crime
	Carefree
Shrewd observers	Bad leaders
Even- Tempered	Unprincipled
Jovial	Disloyal
Excel in career	Easily discouraged
Good soldier	Talkative
Good follower	Flexible/compromising
Nice	

TIMOROUS: THE GOOD POINTS

He is so humble, quiet, slow to anger, simple and long suffering that virtually everybody fights his battles for him. His calm exterior intrigues and serves as lessons to the more aggressive Austere or Caustic. In power, they would take lightly on the Conceit who tries to play on their intelligence or as the case may be. He is generally praised for good character, and when the time comes to nominate the soldier of the month or year as the case may be, he is always the first to be nominated. He does all possible to avoid trouble and carries out all orders. He is a wise planner, spends prudently and an excellent family man. He gives to his family all that is needed psychologically, physically and financially. As he cares for his family, so does he reflect as a leader carrying his soldiers along, working hand in hand with them. No matter his position, he is efficient, reliable and has a diplomatic sense of humor that solves issues resulting in a smile. He is compassionate to the needs of others and careful how he lives his life.

Are you a timorous soldier? Fill in the blanks honestly before reading further.

Timorous- Attributes	What are your weakness
Humble	
Praised for good character	
Discipline	
Loyal	
People fight for them	
Reserved	
Long-suffering	
Slow to anger	
Timid	
Their junior easily rides them	
Hate the spot light	
Scared of change	
Fearful	
Lacks confidence	
Slow	
Social misfit	
Easily influenced	
Misguided loyalist	
Dangerous anger	
Endures hardship	

Value their job

Prudent spenders

Wise planners

Excellent family man

Succumbs to pressure

Low infinity knowledge

Carry people along

Efficiency and reliable

Compassionate

Simple

Peace maker/ diplomatic

Careful

Intensive

Avoid challenges

Fear of failure

Sober

Easy going

Unmotivated

Procrastinator

Hard-working

Talks behind people

TIMOROUS: THE OTHER SIDE

To every up side, there is a down side. The Timorous is too scared of change he will avoid just anything in that direction to remain in his comfort zone. His fear and slow nature have so much effect on his confidence level that sometimes even his juniors ride over him. His superiors over use him and he is mostly influenced by the exigencies of the service, because on his own without being influenced he will not opt for change. He fears failure just as he fears death making him unmotivated and indecisive, procrastinating life decision from day to day, month to month and year to year. He lives a slow and simple life and avoids a challenge; that is why as a rule he hardly exceeds the average life except if luck shines on him because of his humility. He hates the spot light and would not spend money unnecessarily resulting in a non-social life. He has no motivation towards loyalty; he just follows as the trends permit and he is an often victim of Austere and Caustic. He will never air out his grievances to them but complaining continuously in the background. Reanalysis of your shortcomings:

Timorous- strength	Timorous- weakness
Humble	Timid
Praised for good character	Their junior rides them
Discipline	Scared of change
Loyal	Fearful
Slow to anger	Lacks of confidence
Calm exterior	Slow
Endure hardship	Social misfit
Prudent spenders	Easily influenced
Wise planners	Misguided loyalist
Excellent family man	Dangerous anger
Carry people along	Avoid challenges
Efficiency and reliable	Fear of failure
Compassionate	Unmotivated
Hard working	Procrastinator
Peace maker/ diplomatic	talk behind people

PART 4

DEALING WITH THE WEAKNESSES OF THE PERSONALITY TYPES

In the evaluation of the soldier's personality types, we have been reminded of what our strengths are and what may be our weaknesses in a more vivid way. It is not as if we are not aware of this realities, rather it is just that we were never confronted by them like this. It is my opinion that whatever the shortcomings of any personnel are, his strengths lie therein to overcome and overwhelm them. In the understanding of the basic axioms of life irrespective of religious or philosophical association, it is simple fact that the critical issues are survival, preservation of progeny and the continual existence of humankind and its immediate environment. It is not at all different in the life of a soldier, which is ensuring the survival and success of the mission. Our lives and those of our brothers in arms and the preservation of the military might of the country and its progressive growth are the critical issues. In some cases, in other to serve, your life might be required from you. Then it should be accepted that in sacrificing your life you have saved many and supported a great course that is to your country and the Service. This is a stark reality soldiers must embrace first; a reality that should be hammered into their inner minds. That the life and times of a service personnel, the rudiments of the job, the programming of the job ethics, its hierarchy, its tradition and tenets are in a wide margin different from those in the civil life. All these are meant to make us understand that in the long run, our lives might not just be enough. In military history, many soldiers have been sacrificed for a course that is bigger than a single general or a battalion of troops; to wit, a course to unify a country, to quell a rebellion, to restore lost glory etc. In explaining this point, I will use two rules that are the Universal root and the individual root. The universal root is the root of every soldier, his root course that is to serve and sacrifice for his country, while the individual root is what lies in his own mind.

During World War 1 when the Ottoman Empire entered the war, which then seemed stalled on the western front, the allied powers decided to launch a Turkish invasion. This was a naval expedition to seize the Dardanelles straits, a narrow passage connecting the Aegean Sea and the sea of Marmora northwestern Turkey. The capture of the straits would have dealt a big blow on the Axis, thus hastening the end of the war. On March 18, 18 allied ships entered the straits, Turkish fire and undetected mines sank 3 ships and severely damaged three others. Consequently, a failed naval attack led to a large scale troop landing in the Gallipoli peninsula. This all resulted in a catastrophic failure and a failed campaign. In the end, the British government ordered an evacuation. Of 480,000 allied forces that took part in the Gallipoli campaign; they were more than 250,000 causalities' including over 46,000 dead. Emphasis here is on numbers, not just numbers, but people and not just people but soldiers; such is the life of a military personnel. It is in our interest if at all our shortcomings are to be addressed to first come to terms with our reason for being in the Service; not to be sacrificed for but for us to sacrifice even our lives. The men that died in the battles of Gallipoli probably accepted that fact before marching before the enemy. Let us take a closer look home during the Nigerian civil war. On March 31 1968, General Murtala Mohammed was leading a federal military convoy of 96 vehicles carrying logistics and supplies from Enugu to Onitsha and along the way from Abagana; major Ochendu was waiting in ambush leading a guerrilla unit. Of 200 federal troops on that movement over 150 were killed and only about 50 survived with injuries including General Murtala Mohammed. Probably before embarkation, the federal troops would have been confident based on intelligence reports and reconnaissance that the operation was good to go. Who knew on the federal side the bitter end that awaited the 150 soldier that died in that ambush? Of what significance is this point in contrast to the one I explained first? It brings to fore the hazards of the military job, the unexpected circumstances, never conceived that can just sprout taking with it the lives of personnel. Such is the life of a soldier. Risk abounds in all directions whether in peace or wartime. We should accept ourselves for who we are, as soldiers. It should come first before individual ambition to amass wealth, or business connections because irrespective of one's personality, there are all these factors only at different settings. If this reality of what soldering is cannot be accepted, then weakness cannot truly be tamed as it relates to the armed forces. In a previous book I wrote, I emphasized that in bringing harmony and advancement to the armed forces, the human emotion should be tamed. Emotions can trigger human craving, and cravings can distract a soldier from his primary duty. Now let us analyzed this in accordance to personality.

THE AUSTERE

The mind of the austere soldier is influenced by his ambitions, which vary according to individual. The Austere soldier is yet to embrace the universal root of acceptance of his status as a soldier instead of being controlled by his ambitions, which is very dangerous in our line of work. This is because, it only serves as a catalyst to his desire to be selfish, thinking only of himself, something not welcomed in the military service. You are a practical fellow why don't you read the stakes yourself and decide what you want for yourself? Is it your ambitions or to serve your country? If it is your ambition, it is in my opinion that you should put in and face your ambitions squarely and if it is to serve, you should make your service to your country as primary before any other attachments. When you have changed your mindset, you now see things differently than you did before. Now observe with me, if before your ambition is primary to the universal root, your relationship with your colleagues and superiors will be influenced by your ambitions. A relationship of no permanent friend and no permanent enemy, where you use your colleagues strategically to achieve your end; and once they prove useless; you turn your back on them; and if necessary you will betray them. But if your mind set is modified to the universal root, in what light would you see your colleagues and superiors? Now ponder on those people you used to achieve your goals, how do they feel? How will they describe you? Would they want you to use them tomorrow? When the chips are down, what happens? For it cannot be rainy for you all through when the going gets tough who and where will you run to for solace? Disloyalty and betrayal are not the ways of a soldier, because of the rudiments of our job. Think about it, if truly you are as smart as you claim you are, would you not embrace the universal root?

Money and properties will pass, and are all described as vanities, why go to the extreme to achieve them. It is the way of the Austere to go diabolical in order to balance the three aspects' of his life which are business, family and service. In doing these, they affect others negatively. But the Austere should also understand that irrespective of the universal root, there is nemesis that creeps up slowly on the wicked and devilish. It is in my opinion that the Austere should lead a spiritual life while embracing the universal root.

THE CAUSTIC

The Caustic is one that has embraced the universal root and is more than willing to die for it. His weakness stems from the individual root. Are you a Caustic? Sit with me in this dialogue as we contemplate the way forward. You are a much disciplined personality; you have a high percentage of what you need to actualize your dreams, to become a better person for the remaining part of your life. Ok, those are some cool stuff; but is it true that most of the time things do not turn out well for you? Can it be because you have a pessimistic idea of life? Do you sincerely feel you should be optimistic with life; giving to life what you want from it, being positive about all you do and feeling free to express your personality without pretense? Ever since you have been displaying outward perfectionism, how has it helped you moved forward? Rather, are people watching out for you, and waiting for you to make a mistake, so they can blow it in your face? What is the opinion of your family about you? Do they see you as a good pretender? For you, does charity begin at home? What conclusions have you drawn so far? Think and look inward; has it not become necessary to throw away those pasts that hurt, those pasts that want to carve a dreadful future for you? Is the standard you set for yourself same with the one you set inside (within your family)? Have you seen when a man is given an award for outstanding character and his family refuses to identify with him in receiving such award? To the family it may be a mistake, they do not think he deserves it, but on a fair note he actually deserves it. You have to learn to balance work and family and change your two faced lifestyle.

Are you a listener or a talker? Do you enjoy carrying rumors of the bad deeds of others? Have you ever contemplated that one day it will be your turn? As you celebrate other people's lapses, you should also understand that you are not perfect. You are a human being, a mortal and you are bound to make mistakes. So why are you fast in criticizing others? If your close friends were to give you an award, what do you think it will be?

As a Caustic, you are specialized and strong willed. Why not take advantage of your specialty and will, to build a better caustic for you? You cannot change who you are, but you can improve your personality, by doing that you can invest in your family. Be more simplistic about life and drawing people closer rather than pushing them away; because if you continue as you are on retirement you might end up alone. Is that what you want? Definitely not; remember the change you inspire now might be your only source of happiness in your old age.

THE CONCEIT

The Conceit soldier has come to terms with his universal role as a soldier, rating, or an aircraftman and he is proud of his rank and status no matter how small or demeaning it might be. He is ready to defend the integrity of the service and its reputation. He is indeed a poster soldier but his shortcoming presents itself in his lifestyles which in most cases lead to a retirement of failure and continuous regret. In the case of a Conceit, I will hinge on the individual root and the need to differentiate between reality and fiction. One of the many outstanding sides of the Repressed is their ability to have a good sense of reality irrespective of anything else. They know their limits in all aspects especially finance. What a Conceit should realize is that life in the service is quite different from life after service, and that is what they should be concerned. As far as the military service is concerned about 80 percent of the things they pursue workout in their favor. This is because of their manipulative and lobbying skills, or their parent who may have been retired personnel or sheer luck. But after service, all these would change, that is why it is imperative for the Conceit soldier to begin now to plan for retirement.

As a Conceit soldier, you are probably the person with all the latest gadgets, the newest trends are known to you. This makes your lifestyle luxurious and extravagant compared to your income. Now think about it really; is this your reality? Can you say honestly to yourself without any self-doubt that you have no regrets in the fake life you are living? How long do you want to follow the trend of things in vogue? And can you survive on your basic salary if you continue? Is there a competition between you and another person? Who is the judge if at all there is? And lastly what can you possibly gain and what will be the result if you continue like this till retirement? Ask yourself these questions, write down your answers, reflect on them and decide on these.

Are you willing for the sake of your future to cut down on your set standards in life? To face reality squarely and spend based on your income? Are you willing to save on your own instead of waiting for dubious markets that bring stocks that often never appreciate to your office before you can invest? Are you ready to put aside your pride and embrace humility because pride goes before a fall? Are you ready to spend your money to acquire knowledge in education instead of buying fanciful things? If you have made up your mind to take these steps you should start today because as it is well known, a stitch in time saves nine. Set your target and pursue it tenaciously, think about a fruitful end and how it will boost your ego. Begin to save for your future today and you will not end up like the man who studied abroad, became a renowned journalist, earned good money, married wives, and the only house he acquired as at the time was in his girlfriend's name. What a pitiful story; too pitiful for the fragile ego of the regular Conceit. Is that what you want for yourself? A situation where your children will have no connection to you and are just waiting for you to die because you are of no use to them? Spend wisely today and save and plan for tomorrow to ensure a promising future.

THE EUPHORIC

First I would like to appeal to the military authorities, requesting that instead of trying to manage the euphoric soldier which over time has not yielded enduring results, rehabilitation Centre's should be established. Such Centre's should have clinical psychologists who can talk to these soldiers and help them address the issues that push them to drink constantly, and confine also those with drug habits. To this effect, I believe a remarkable change can be accomplished.

On a lighter note, I have questions for the euphoric soldier. Do people easily give up on you? Has your family written you off? Does the world regard you as a person of shame and filth? Then Congratulations, you are reading this book because it is the first step to change that status of yours and prove the world wrong! Your weaknesses may obviously overwhelm your strength. Irrespective of whether or not you have embraced the universal root, things are going to get better for you if you are willing to accept change and work on your personality. To do this, you will climb three steps.

STEP ONE: if you are still single, Marry, a decent and God fearing woman, because your immediate family has a whole lot to play in your present and future. For those that are married the next steps will help you straighten things out.

STEP TWO: Be visionary, learn to look beyond today. There is something called tomorrow and today was the tomorrow of 'the yesterday' that you were talking about, and now that you cannot change that past, learn to leave the past in the past, it is the future you have to change, and today is the best time for you to start changing the future. Start by picking a role model in the service. Someone you admire and respect and who has an interest in you and your family and will give you the appropriate advice at any point in time. Enough of the service threatening you and your excesses;

cell days is not now; the time for your debtors to embarrass you on the road should end. Now is the time to plan for your family and your life. Make haste while the sun yet shines. Today you might be tolerated in the service because they have come to terms with who you are, but there comes a time, if you continue in your ways, when the service will get tired of tolerating you and dismiss you. Is that the period you want to plan? Is that when you will beg your Commander that you will change? Why not become visionary from today and prove the world wrong!

STEP THREE: Cut down on your excesses, that are the third step to your desired change, your intake of alcohol. Your debt habit, your discipline issues, must be considered. For instance, if you normally have disciplinary issues every month, please be cautious and cut it down to at least ones in two months or in three months. Forget about prostitutes and go for decent women, be moderate about everything and cut down on being a talkative. If you usually spend 1000 naira on alcohol split it into two for a start, use one for the alcohol and save half either with your wife or where you cannot easily touch it. Continue like this and worry not; a little step at a time you will get there.

When you have now followed the three steps what remains is for you to draw your attention to your children if you have. Make sure there are not backwards in the midst of their equal in school and at home. Do not collect your last entitlement and spend on whores and beer parlors; do something tangible with it. And whenever you have issues with decision consult your service model figure, he will sure put you through. And always remember a decent wife is key to your desired change; choose wisely.

THE REPRESSED

The Repressed needs to come to terms with the universal root, which is to accept that his status as a soldier is not an everyday job to feed his family and solve his problems. To the Repressed, the job is just a means of survival to him, since he probably had a family before being recruited. The original mind set of the Repressed is inhibited by many factors in his life which he has now come to terms with and aligned them with his being. The factors are the suffering he experienced in the past, the deprivation as a child and the constant changes that hampered his life. These are the circumstances that pushed him into service, not a calling to serve or a willing decision to enlist. The need to appeal to circumstance is what majorly pushed the Repressed to join the service. It is the appeal to circumstance that influences his actions even in the service, bringing out his weakness, because his true self is repressed by circumstances and he had the wrong idea on enlistment into the military service. These same circumstances reflect themselves in his way of life, because the Repressed is prone to have a lot of family and financial issues which make him a mediocre in life. What then is the individual root of the Repressed soldier? His circumstances! Alas for the Repressed, good news abound; for the roots of the past can be hewn down swiftly with a transformation of the mindset which influences their actions. This can be done by replacing the latter root of circumstances with the universal root of understanding your place as a soldier. This way, the Repressed understands that he does not need to bow down to everybody because he is scared of a trial. He only needs to act within the purview of military and civil laws. He also learnt that his actions would not now appeal to an irrational fear attached to his past failure and sufferings. But it will appeal to an ultimate goal of serving the armed forces of his country while he supports his immediate family which should be his priority. Those are who the military is concerned about and know as your family. Pushing yourself to support an extended lot will only reduce your efficiency as a soldier, which is now your individual root. It cannot be allowed to stand, where applicable lend your support and if not, state clearly your status. Your appearance should not also inhibit your social expression. Even though you look older than the age you profess and also your rank, you should muster courage and understand that to be a good soldier you must be confident in who you are. By doing this, engage in other activities the service has set for the purpose of making you a better soldier. In certain cases, as regards sociality, the Repressed always have a fantasy towards the social status of the Conceit and indeed join them sometimes to socialize. Now for the Repressed that has had such experience, ponder on what lessons is learnt on such engagement. Of course, there is a lesson to be learnt there because even in the bar, a Conceit will still talk about rank and seniority that is how far their love for the job stretches.

Do you realize that you are a resourceful soldier as you are creative? But you are too scared to venture, too scared to invest but you should always know that life gives back to you what you give to it. Open your mind and learn to be optimistic about life irrespective of your past failures and mistakes. Let your aspirations in being a fulfilled soldier both in the field and at home guard your actions, let it be your focus for it is the only ingredient you need to be a leading soldier, rating or aircraftman.

THE SERVICE-CHAMELEON

The Service-Chameleon has probably made up his mind to serve, that is he has accepted the universal root, but he has a reservation that is restricted to serving or supporting a course that is thriving. It is in these that his major flaws come to play and these are prompted by his constant need to be elevated in the eyes of other soldiers and even civilians. These are the factors that influence the majority of his decisions as it relates to the service. He is a people's person who wants to please people and be seen as an important entourage in the league of the winning team. On his own, he hates to be at the fore front but likes to take second place to have a visible successful mentor. What a life? And the most difficult antecedent of the

Service-Chameleon is that they will never accept that this is who they are. Well the worst thing you can ever do to yourself is to lie to 'yourself'; and I mean you! Because without accepting yourself for who you are, there is no change. Have you accepted that this is who you are? If you have, that is the first step to change for a better future and a fruitful retirement without regrets. Your adapting skills are a plus especially in the military, but you have to learn to channel it positively, not adapting or mimicking for the sake of recognition or prestige but as your duties require. Learn to stay true to your masters irrespective of what the times are telling, do not reflect loyalty as a means to an end but do with integrity. Do away with vain praises as even those you praise are careful of you. Give complement where necessary and do not let your actions be prompted by the crowd. Understand and come to terms with what you really want out of life and stay true to its whether it is popular or not. Lastly, never live your life in reflection of others; it is an error without a price tag; learn to take charge on your own, and see how others will flock around you because you already have the potentials.

THE TIMOROUS

The Timorous has drawn a line; he has built a barricade around himself; a fence he will not jump except confronted with life threatening cases or endowed with limitless power which is rare. The barricade he has built is his fear that is his major weakness. Sometimes it is a sub-conscious effort to avoid trouble, confrontation or face his own short comings as his mind has built a wall. Whatever is not within the walls means he will have to extend a limit which he does not have the mental resources to confront. These are what brings out the offensive path of him; his inhibition to express his grievances to superior or instruct his subordinates making him a gossiper who talks and grumbles behind their backs because he is scared of a confrontations. Same trend makes him a misguided loyalist almost all he does is influenced by the wall he has built. The Timorous needs to break that wall, destroy that barricade and have absolute control of his emotion and limitations. If any personality needs a wall, it's not a Timorous. How possible is this? I will give one answer- 'he needs to disbelieve a lie and see the truth'. Because believe it or not, what keeps those walls holding is a simple lie that those walls are his saving grace, that they have kept him from trouble and as such will continue to keep him safe, when in actual reality those walls are holding him back, holding his true self from expressing itself. Life is too short for such an expensive mistake. There is a saying that goes... for you to truly own something, you must be willing first to lose it. The Timorous should learn to let go of his comfort zone, because for him to be able to achieve anything, he must first learn to be self-confident believing in himself and his abilities to make a difference through his own idea and dreams. Learning to appreciate what springs forth from his inside. I recall a tale where a son followed his father to the bank to cash some money, and when the cashier handed the money to the man his son quickly snatch the money and said his father couldn't count. The man stood dumb founded as the son counted the money and handed it to him incomplete. On reaching outside the father picked a quarrel with the boy and inquired the reasons behind his action only to realize that the man can count the money but does not want people to laugh at how many times he will recount. This explains in details the issues the Timorous endures because he will not cross the wall he has built. Another situation is where a parade is mustered and a detail is to be issued to a single soldier, in most cases the Timorous just volunteers even though his junior is present there. The Timorous also have an issue with distraction, uncertainty of their goals and objectives. Instead he needs to fix his eyes on his goal, and do not wait for the whistle before he starts the race of his life. In order for his dreams to be accomplished, he needs to not be taught to save but rather to learn to avoid distractions, saying yes when necessary and no when it is needed without holding back.

PART 5

PERSONALITY TYPES IN LOYALTY AND SERVICE TO COUNTRY AND ARMED FORCES

The life of military personnel is a life dedicated to service in its utmost form. First, service to country, service to his arm of the armed forces either the Army, Navy or the Air force, service to your command, ship, unit or establishment, to your commanding officer and so on. On enlistment into the service there is the attestation to serve loyally without a bias mind even giving our very lives for our country and service. Over the years, such service to country has been carried out through variety of channels befitting each personnel. On smaller cases, landmarks have been made in such services to glory of country and armed forces in general. However, in recent times, due to factors relating to economic and the general state of things, the military service is now mostly coveted not for service but as a means of employment. It is true you cannot serve two masters at the same time, for every personnel who sees the military job as a means to an end, carries in mind this mindset which precedes his need to serve. Altering output and efficiency in ways inconceivable mostly unknown to the conscious mind; but it is a fact that more than 50% of personnel in the armed forces were obligated to join owing to lack of employment in other areas. Factors like these are what should be considered in handling personnel, because the output of the military determines the stability of a country and the output of the military is highly, depended of the efficiency of its personnel, their dedication to work and their loyalty to the country. It is a huge factor I would advise the leadership of the country to check in relation to employment and the military authority in relation to recruitment and enlistment. The mind set of person on enlistment is a critical factor inasmuch as we enjoy peacetimes, one must prepare for war in other to experience peace. The military strength of any country is highly dependent not even on the officers but on the men. A disloyal band of solders would give the toughest General a hard time. In most cases, a soldier is obligated to leave the family and loved ones behind for years, putting his mind into the battle or operation ahead. In general sense, the life of a soldier during service is a life of sacrifice and the efficiency of such sacrifice is highly dependent on the will of whoever is involved in the scenario in any case. Such will, will be described in two categories on how it applies with personality.

- **On personal capacity with officers**
- **Military operation / vocations**

PERSONAL CAPACITY WITH OFFICERS

As an officer progresses in his career in the military, his relationship with other ranks becomes strained by many factors some of which are his busy schedule, the responsibility of command, his office and the need to observe from distance which is peculiar to leadership qualities. Another is the need to appear capable and strong before his men not reflecting certain emotions of weakness etc. All these are factors that come with authority, either as the head of department, a commanding officer etc. Now, every military commander or head of department is a distant observer no matter how condescending he might attempt to be, it is often difficult to understand fully the scheme of things as relate to his men. What mostly determines this are the soldiers around him, the one closest to him either as a personal assistant, orderly, driver, steward, cook as the case may be. The mind set of such people is important in determining the kind of information that is relayed to officers with actual power, because such information form an important part of whatever they compare and contrast in making decision that affect the country, their service, command and their career. It then becomes imperative to be careful on the type of people that are detailed to officers both in their houses and in offices.

Now let's describe each personality types and what their possible output might be on personal capacity with officers.

THE AUSTERE

The peculiar factor of every personality is what is often most domineering in his psychological output influencing his decisions. For the Austere, some of those peculiar factors are his ambition, need for power and control either through his financial standing or status in the armed forces, his interest in elevating himself in whatever direction he chooses either as a business man, an educational elite, or an outstanding soldier etc. These needs are what lie at the top of his motivation and which influence his every output.

Before an Austere personnel will work willingly for an officer, his working with such officer must have supported any of the notions I mentioned above. Austere are objective and strategic because they often know what they want and have the will to get it and will reflect itself on who they work with, their actions and inactions are prompted by their personal ambition which is the catalyst to their loyalty. They are hardly loyal, if they feign it, it is just a means to an end and the moment the position, authority, status, or appointment of such officers is not benefiting to their overall plan again, they will tactically look for an excuse to withdraw themselves. If the goal of an Austere aligns itself with the visions of a commander of his command, he becomes the best he can be and his output is often excellent. It is relative to blends of Austere that take pleasure in their specialization. An educationally inclined Austere will work and be loyal to an educationally inclined officer. Austere are efficient once their dreams coincide with those of the commander, or the commander is willing to actively support their dreams. When imposed on an officer against their will, these types know the road-map on how to frustrate the job of whoever they are detailed to serve, until they are relieved of such assignments. Such expressions are carried out with practical objectivity which is to end such unproductive assignment in relation to their personal goals.

THE EUPHORIC

Giving the background and the lifestyle of a basic Euphoric, they hardly work with officers; neither will you find them in sensitive offices. They are mostly used as sentries or operations befitting their Euphoric status. The Euphoric is a soldier that is managed by the authority as a result of the outcomes of his euphoric nature.

THE CAUSTIC

A Caustic soldier has many relations to an average bile temperament; but not entirely, even easygoing people end up being Caustic. But a notable thing about this personality is that their bile is always more than enough and its fuel never runs dry. Normally, a Caustic soldier will like to work with a rational General or officer; a rigid and cruel enforcer that is if given the opportunity to pick. And as I explained earlier that every Caustic has a course in his mind whether consciously or sub-consciously, a wrong that touched their lives through childhood that they feel should be corrected or something in their physicality that they consider a disability in all totality. A pushing factor, a catalyst that influences most things they do; that is what forms the paradigm through which they see life and the military service. This is because no matter how hard they try, it is difficult to hide from an observer, because the Caustic is generally expressive, and this expressive nature, if on personal capacity with a commander or officer is determined by the commander or officer involved. A caustic soldier can sacrifice even the happiness of his family for a stern commander who he believes in and who gives him power to impose his will or rewrite what he sees as wrong. He betrays any soldier, close friends, associate to support the will of his commander or officer. He will preach the gospel of his commander or officer to anybody that cares to listen; such is his service when he is given the full power and authority and when the officer involved is a stern officer. But if the officer expresses or believes in diplomacy; managing the wrong of his men instead of punishment, it becomes obvious that his ideals and advice will be repressed, and his loyalty to the commander or officer will be on face value. On his own, he will complain about his weakness and the wrong of his ways; and how military discipline is falling behind; in some cases, if he enjoys monetary gift from the commander or officer he might not be openly expressive but those close to him will always get a wind of his ideal and how it does not tally with his commander. Such will affect his efficiency because he will just work for working sake; not putting in too much and embracing the ideal that the job is not 'finish and go'. To a Caustic soldier money and gift can only make him smile more, grumble less on face value; but his overall loyalty and the efficiency of his output to his commander or officer as the case may be is highly dependent on the sternness or rigidity of the commander or officer and the level of leash he gives to the Caustic.

THE CONCEIT

The ideal that forms the paradigm through which a Conceit views life and his military service are ones involving a high level of perfectionism, devotion to the military job and reflection of same in all respects. The Conceit loves his comfort zone; where his ideal and pride will not be trampled upon and where social life will not be inhabited. In spite of all this, the Conceit has an active conscience whereby irrespective of the ideals of a commander or officer he will hardly do anything to jeopardize his job. They like to justify their actions; to seem civilized and reasonable and only in cases of extreme maltreatment, then you will see them protest. And when they do, they make sure it goes public; sometimes for the superior of which ever officer is involved to get a wind of; and when I say protest I do not mean banners and street protest. He can jeopardize the work of the commander or officer in such a way that it will not fall back to them legally speaking. He can purposely absent himself from duty with the officer, reporting to a higher authority; he reacts in diverse ways. The Conceit is not really an efficient soldier; most of the things he does are for public sentiment, his reputation and his efficiency sometimes are for that sake. The basic Conceit is unserious both in his personal life and in the service, his seriousness is determined by his pride, so technically he will not do well with a commander or officer who does not share his values; although he will work loyally and with his mind; but when the commander is prone to many activities and is himself a workaholic, the Conceit finds it difficult to meet up. He works better with an officer that shares his value not putting in too much and at the same time doing his primary duties. Like going to the office, closing on time; attend probably one meeting during the week, something like that fits his profile and he will be able to meet up with. But on the other hand, a commander or officer that is activity prone, he will always seem; stressed out; over used; he might not complain about it openly. A Conceit devoted to military service sees grumbling as a civilian thing, it is one of the ideals he upholds; he might find other ways to express his grievance. He is a devoted soldier that in face of an average quantity of work or activity will perform his best loyally.

THE REPRESSED

The lifestyle of the Repressed is mostly influenced by his past struggles, the hardship he endured in life and what it took him before he finally made up his mind to join the service and was eventually selected for training. His primary goal is survival and a service time that is absent of trouble i.e. charges and court-martials, so whatever they do they avoid problem. This trend affects in a high extent their efficiency level because they tend to be mediocre in nature, doing everything on an average level not pushing too hard or going too far just to avoid trouble. As a rule, they have a lot of family problems that affect their output and spending, so when on personal capacity with a commander or an officer they will work averagely with one that meets their needs. You cannot expect a Repressed soldier to perform beyond average except he has a blend of Caustic or Austere. No matter the incentive he gets, he does not put in too much or too less, his devotion is his survival and shelter. On the other hand, in the service and upon retirement, if a Repressed soldier is working with a frugal officer or commander, his idea will be to use his problem to intimidate the commander or the officer till he looks for someone else; he will carry a pitiful face, move slowly when delegated etc.

And for some commanders that find such thing irritating and are forceful, they will end up locking up such soldiers. When being punished, they will tell their very touchy problems to people who care to listen and you will pity them and see the commander as a cruel man. This is because their problems are ones that are touchy, if it even actually exists. They know how to say it without having any personnel pride, discrediting the commander or officer concerned. The Repressed just want to work and collect his salary avoiding hassle or risk to his job or the welfare of his family. Anything that will risk that, he will quickly report to a higher authority or opt-out.

THE SERVICE CHAMELEON

The Service Chameleon naturally likes to be attached to a commander or officer, irrespective of his ideas or appointment. It is a trend that is influenced by their penchant to be perceived as relevant or vital in whatever ship or establishment they serve. And whatever they do in service to the commander or officer is for the preservation of their post. They are mostly at this point not interested in money, if it comes they will consider it a plus, they love the name it gives them, so it is not the fact that there are efficient or will be efficient in their service to such officers. Their efficiency is based on the commander or officer himself; some commanders and officers do not measure personnel attached to them by his efficiency, they just want you to do your basic job and even when you are lacking they might understand enough to overlook. The Service

– Chameleon will measure his output to this level and reflect same to the commander or officer involved. If otherwise and the commander or officer is stern and principled, he will reflect same. The Service – Chameleon is not loyal as a rule, the moment he sees a better opportunity he will excuse himself without blinking, he can even do it sub-consciously. When attached to a commander or officer even without the officer's approval the Service-Chameleon can use his name and appointment to accumulate favors for himself. They are naturally fraudulent and love things in that respect. They are good at carrying out such act and covering it up. Their words, actions, inactions and level of efficiency are measured by what they perceive is the possible expectation of the commander or officer involved. They reflect the ideas of the commander or officer even in their personal lives, it's in their nature and it determines their efficiency.

THE TIMOROUS

The Timorous has certain similarities with the Repressed in relationship to work output and efficiency. The difference is that their actions, is not determined or influenced by past struggles or suffering neither is their efficiency level regulated by only the need to survive. The Timorous is naturally calm and gentle and does not want trouble. His need to get the job done, carrying his duties without penalties, charges or court martial is not primarily for the protection of his job or that he sees the job as his only hope. It is out of an impulse to do things right to avoid hostility, trouble and heightened activities that will put him in the spotlight. The Timorous is most fearful amongst the personality types and his high level of fear inhibits, to a large extent, his level of efficiency. Nevertheless, with pressure or under the influence of a pushy superior, he overcomes his fears and becomes more efficient. When in service to commander or senior officer, he reflects same attributes and is always loyal and obedient; but personally he will not allow his loyalty to affect his relationship with other personnel. However, if it does eventually, as a defense he quickly blames it on the commander or officer he is attached to. He hardly takes responsibility for his actions; he prefers to be in the background. He can be a good and effective soldier to work with. With a little push, he becomes more efficient showing loyalty even in the face of maltreatment and not distinguishing what job is military and which is not. He carries out his orders without complaint or grumbling to the commander or officer involved. It takes him a long time before he confronts his superior on such matter where he feels he is wrongly treated or where he feels he can no longer endure such mistreatment and want to leave. And at that point he has finally made up his mind, he hardly goes back. He expects whoever he works with to know his needs and the limit of work load he can endure without him voicing out his opinion. A downside to the loyalty and obedience of the Timorous is that he is susceptible to influences. His will is fragile and can be broken under a forceful influence.

PERSONALITY TYPES AND MILITARY VOCATIONS

It might seem alarming but to every personality there is vocation of service specialization that best suits their bearing. In our distinct nature as human beings we have come to fore, to a plain understanding that we have gifts, and talents that vary from one person to another. And when blended with what is at the top of our intellectual output, we become the best we can be, even without extensive training. Same can be applied to the personality types and the various vocations that are available in the military. Just like an introverted melancholic will be a better artist, than an extroverted choleric, so a dedicated Service-Chameleon will be a better armorer than your average Repressed. Thus it becomes necessary to know that to every specialization there is a recommended personality that best suits it for efficiency and effectiveness.

THE AUSTERE

The Austere is as a rule objective, strategic and practical, displaying a high level of business acumen and keen sense in developing his mental mind in whatever vocation is primary to him. This makes him most effective as construction personnel, avionics, electrician maintenance personnel, engineering science, technical professionals and administrative personnel.   As most Austere are, if not clever, smart and if not smart, brilliant displaying a high level of intuition and putting attention to details in whatever is their priority. The Austere is also a good judge of character can portray images to fit public light and can be a good enforcer which makes him skilled in human resources, media and public affairs (military public relations and journalism), physical training personnel and provost personnel. As a chaplain, an Austere also does well because a morally inclined Austere is one that does not like corruption or sin.

THE CAUSTIC

The Caustic is strong-willed and loves to be where the action is, not just for him to be there, but they have a high propensity for violence well fitted for combat personnel (Special Forces, infantry, artillery, seamen, operation of tanks and other combat machinery). Caustics are also good judges of character, supporters of authority and active enforcers, hence they will make good provost personnel, human resources specialist, physical training personnel; a morally inclined Caustic will also make a good chaplain.

THE CONCEIT

Amongst the personality types the Conceit is one to have accepted his status as a soldier, welcoming combat no matter how life threatening it might sound making him a devoted combat personnel. The Conceits are mostly brilliant and will do well in engineering science, avionics equipment specialists, technical professionals, health care professionals as they can be compassionate and understanding of human pain and also as administrative personnel. They will also do well as human resources specialists, media and public affair as they are good at public relations, physical training personnel, and transport and material handling considering that a Conceit is the personality with the highest level of integrity.

THE EUPHORIC

A singular specialization that suits the Euphoric is combat, given their euphoric nature it is the only specialization that they can manage without excessive setbacks as a result of their characteristics. As a combat personnel, a Euphoric can still be seen as lacking if he is expose to excessive doses of drugs and alcohol. However, his Euphoric status is useful in certain military operations that the sanity of a man must be absent in other to achieve the desired outcome.

THE REPRESSED

The Repressed before enlistment mostly have already learnt a trade or hand work and can be related to either being –mechanics, construction personnel, electrical maintenance. And considering their Repressed status, they have a high tendency towards mediocrity and their pride level is low and a job as that of cook or steward require humility and devotion. They will also perform well as chaplains and transport material/handling personnel.

THE SERVICE- CHAMELEON

The Service-Chameleon is a natural adapter, quick learner and an intuitive survivor; characters essential for a combat personnel (Special Forces, infantry, artillery, seamen, operation of tanks and other combat machinery). He can also be rated as the best personality in the combat branch, in operation that involves direct confrontation with hostile forces. Additionally, they are quick learners and are good with machinery and can operate tanks and other combat machinery as navigators, gun boat drivers etc. They also perform well as media and public affairs & physical training personnel.

THE TIMOROUS

Given the calm and diplomatic nature of Timorous, they make good administrative personnel, because of their patience and carefulness with records. They also make good construction personnel, avionics equipment specialist, electrical maintenance personnel, engineering science and technical professionals, health care professionals, mechanics, cook, steward, Chaplin and transport/ handling of materials. The Timorous can be versatile, his inborn nature and personality best suit these service vocation.

When it comes to combat work, it is in fact the primary duty of every soldier, rating or aircraftman, but they are certain personalities that are not just suited for such jobs. Let's take the Repressed for example;

the Repressed soldier is always carried away, his mind is always wondering, not good at all for combat-work because a distracted soldier is a dead soldier. In most cases of miss fire, it is often recorded with Repressed because they can hardly bring their mind to the job at hand, which can be devastating for the morale of the entire troops. The Timorous is naturally fearful, his fear is dangerous for combat operations, especially when it involves hostile forces, his fear can capitulate into a state of general confusion, distracting other soldiers and impeding the operation in general. The Timorous and Repressed are also not confident in their ability and it inhibits their movement in the field and such self-doubt can lead to death and failure eventually. On the battle field, hesitation for a moment can foil an entire operation that has taken years to plan. For the Austere, in most cases he is a selfish soldier prone to personal elevation of self and status; such imbedded mentality is not needed on the battle field. Soldiers have to work together "one for all and all for one" entering danger and life threatening spots to ensure the survival of a fellow soldier or the overall success of the mission. All the personality blends explained have a tendency both towards fear and repression but the levels always vary according to personality types and repression is highest in the Repressed personality. They have the highest tendency towards mediocrity. In the Conceit and Austere, their repressed status is inhibited by stronger traits of egotism and self-confidence. The job description of a soldier, a rating or aircraftman generally promotes the feeling of mediocrity, the feeling of being an other rank or an inferior. Such influence has been imbedded and accepted by many personnel which in reality are not what is supposed to be imbedded; not mediocrity or an inferiority complex, but a need to come to teams, that our existence is rated in a hierarchical order in accordance to the general scheme of things which then translates to service to our country. And as we continue to grow in this, we continue to accept ourselves for who we are, not what history or our status terms us to be. Such trend and mentality need to be quelled by the military high authority in order to lesson cases of indiscipline and indiscriminate behaviors, unbecoming of service personnel and to promote in general the efficiency of every soldier, rating and aircraft man who see themselves as inferior and hence behave as such. In that way, the military service would be viewed on a more elevated note and a reputation befitting such an esteemed and important organ of the country will be accorded it.